"In a cultural environment where religion is often used to enhance one's identity, John Martens's *The Word on the Street* is a good example of what Pope Francis called 'theology on one's knees.' Doing theology begins with Scripture and worship: in this sense, a book of Sunday reflections for the liturgical year stands at the center, at the beginning, and the end of what nurtures the Christian experience, beyond the different liturgical and political commitments that divide the Church today. But John Martens's book is far from indifferent to the meaning of Scripture for the life of Christians in the world of today."

— Massimo Faggioli, professor of theology and religious studies at Villanova University (Philadelphia)

"Every week at *America* magazine, I wait with eager anticipation to see what John Martens is going to say about the Gospel for the coming Sunday or Feast Day. And I am never, ever, disappointed. Firmly grounded in the latest Scripture scholarship, wonderfully practical, and beautifully written, his reflections always teach me something new. Martens is that rare scholar that can write well for the general audience, and, even rarer, say something new."

— James Martin, SJ, author of *Jesus: A Pilgrimage*

"John Martens is not only an excellent biblical scholar, he also has a pastor's soul. These weekly reflections help us get inside the scriptures each Sunday in a way that is scholarly, accessible, and spiritually rich. He makes the Word of God alive in so many thoughtful ways. This volume is a perfect synthesis of heart and mind, a place I can go to learn about the biblical readings for each week, be touched by God and grow spiritually. I enthusiastically recommend *The Word on the Street* for all Christians, from thoughtful high school and college students to lay adults of all ages, and even (and especially) to theologians. Each reflection has something for everyone."

— Peter Feldmeier, Murray/Bacik Endowed Professor of Catholic Studies, University of Toledo

THE WORD ON THE STREET

Year B

Sunday Lectionary Reflections

JOHN W. MARTENS

LITURGICAL PRESS

Collegeville, Minnesota

www.litpress.org

1   2   3   4   5   6   7   8   9

Library of Congress Cataloging-in-Publication Data

Names: Martens, John W., 1960– author.
Title: The word on the street : Year B : Sunday lectionary reflections / John W. Martens.
Description: Collegeville, Minnesota : Liturgical Press, 2017.
Identifiers: LCCN 2017027378 (print) | LCCN 2017009938 (ebook) | ISBN 9780814649886 (ebook) | ISBN 9780814649633
Subjects: LCSH: Church year meditations. | Bible—Meditations. | Catholic Church—Prayers and devotions. | Catholic Church. Lectionary for Mass (U.S.). Year B.
Classification: LCC BX2170.C55 (print) | LCC BX2170.C55 M3425 2017 (ebook) | DDC 242/.3—dc23
LC record available at https://lccn.loc.gov/2017027378

contents

preface

For those who read the Bible as the word of God, it is a properly daunting task to write on the Scripture. God's word has been given to us for our salvation, to allow us to order our lives properly and to grow in holiness, which is to grow to be more and more like God. As the apostle Paul urged the Thessalonians, "we ask and urge you in the Lord Jesus that, as you learned from us how you ought to live and to please God (as, in fact, you are doing), you should do so more and more" (1 Thess 4:1). That is, to grow in holiness is a continuing process and so, too, is reading and understanding the Bible. It is a task that is never finished, in which new insights and developments continue to emerge. To be able to speak authoritatively on the Scripture, therefore, ought not to be an act of hubris, but an act of humility, reflection, and prayer in which God is allowed to speak to us and direct us.

The writings you find here are mostly the products of a weekly process in which I spent time thinking about and praying with the readings for each Sunday, and pondering the things of my life, both ordinary and extraordinary, as I constructed my columns for *America* magazine's The Word and then returned to them and revised each of them as I prepared this book. A number of reflections, ten in total, have also been prepared specifically for this edition and have not appeared in *America* previously. The same processes, however, lie behind these writings.

It is a humbling task not just because I am writing on Scripture, but because I am aware of how many people have read the columns and will read this book, hoping to gain spiritual guidance, sustenance, and inspiration, and how many great scholars have written the column for *America* magazine in the previous years and decades. But then one adds to this the fact that some of the greatest minds ever have been writing on Scripture throughout the ages, such as St. Jerome, St. Augustine, St. Thomas Aquinas . . . and it is enough to make you throw down your quill (or keyboard) and wonder what you have to add.

And at this point, Scripture comes to our aid once again. You realize that the Bible is written for every age and it needs to be heard anew by every person and that task will fall on some of us in every era. Paul claimed that he was "the least of the apostles, unfit to be called an apostle, because I persecuted the church of God. But by the grace of God I am what I am, and his grace toward me has not been in vain" (1 Cor 15:9-10). I am not comparing myself to Paul, but I am suggesting that each of us has a call that, even when we feel unworthy of it, God gives us the ability to fulfill. Paul went on to say that "I worked harder than any of them— though it was not I, but the grace of God that is with me" (1 Cor 15:10). I cannot say that I worked harder than anyone, but I can say that these columns emerge from my long training in biblical studies, my desire to grasp God's word, and my willingness to sit with the Bible, in English, Greek, and Hebrew, and to deliberate over each word, in order to answer a call I was not certain I was capable of fulfilling. More and more, I realize it is God's grace that enables the hard work and the skills that I claim as my own.

It is here, too, where I must thank my colleagues at *America* magazine, especially James Martin, SJ, Matt Malone, SJ, Bob Collins, SJ, Tim Reidy, Kerry Weber, and many others, who persevered in order to give me the opportunity to write the column, and who encouraged me along the way and did the hard work of editing my columns every week. They allowed me the freedom to write on Scripture in whatever context emerged for that week and gave me unfailing support on whatever path I chose. In the same way, I wish to thank my editors at Liturgical Press for giving me this opportunity and shepherding it from start to finish with such professional care.

I also must thank my parents, John and Gertrude Martens, for instilling in me a great love of Scripture, which was cemented in the Mennonite church in which I grew up and by a large extended family on both my mother's and father's sides of the family. I grew up in an environment thoroughly drenched in Scripture, which was not seen as a dead letter but as a living word that had been enacted, for instance, in bringing my family from the horrors of Stalinist Soviet Union to the refugee camps of post– World War II Europe and then to Canada. They did not and do not see these events as accidental, but as signs of God's providence. This is how they continue to read and interpret the Bible: it impacts our day-to-day lives and makes sense of them, giving them meaning and purpose.

Real interpretation of Scripture takes place at the ground level, in how we live our lives, and no one has helped me shape my interpretation of Scripture more than my own family, Tabitha, Sam, and Jake, who have aided me not just to think and to write about the Bible, but have challenged me to live out the Scripture every day, at street level.

Finally, however, I wish to thank all of you, the readers, who have sent numerous emails and handwritten letters (yes, readers send handwritten letters in envelopes still!) to encourage and support me every week. It is for the readers that this book is titled *The Word on the Street*. It is not intended to indicate a kind of hip knowingness about the ways of the world, but to indicate that Scripture is intended to speak to us where we live, whether the street, the suburbs, refugee camps, the big city, or the farm, and to meet us in our daily lives. Wherever you are and whatever stage of life you are in, God has something to say to you through the word of God. I am thankful that I can participate in this work and thank God for allowing this opportunity to speak with you. I hope you enjoy reading this book as much as I have enjoyed writing it and I hope this book enables you to encounter God, the source of all true joy, in Scripture and on the street, as you go about your lives ordinary and extraordinary, certain in the knowledge that God is with you.

John W. Martens

Daily Distractions

First Sunday of Advent

Readings: Isa 63:16b-17, 19b; 64:2-7; Ps 80:2-3, 15-16, 18-19;
1 Cor 1:3-9; Mark 13:33-37

"Beware, keep alert; for you do not know when the time will come."
(Mark 13:33)

Pope Francis said, on World Environment Day, June 5, 2013, "We are losing our attitude of wonder, of contemplation, of listening to creation . . . Why do we think and live horizontally, we have drifted away from God, we no longer read his signs" (General Audience, St. Peter's Square). He was referring to the physical environment, but he links the lack of awareness of our physical surroundings, nature, and the human milieu to inattentiveness and distraction concerning the spiritual world. If we do not attend carefully to the things of this world, including ourselves, we lose sight of God.

During Advent we need to refocus our spiritual attention. One way we can do this is to gently question our need for instant gratification and quick answers in all areas of life. How many of us today are bound by our smartphones, responding thoughtlessly by reaching for our phones whenever we hear email or direct message tings, regardless of what we are doing or with whom we are talking? Our devices follow us everywhere, not allowing us time to think or reflect.

We are losing the sense of wonder and contemplation, unable to read the signs of the times because of distractedness. This has an impact on our prayer, sense of community and family, and spiritual reflection. Distraction has permeated our daily lives so completely that intellectual, spiritual, and emotional focus can no longer be taken for granted. Distractedness does not allow us to wait; it does not allow for patience, for it wants what it wants now.

Constant access to information and sources of knowledge is not a substitute for wisdom. It can, however, draw us into the mire of minutiae,

1

away from real thinking, wonder, and contemplation, and lead us to ignore our need to wait patiently to be prepared to encounter Christ. Patient waiting is neither distracted nor empty behavior. Patient waiting allows us to contemplate our lives and consider how we will prepare to greet the coming of Christ during Advent, to wonder about the signs of God and what they are speaking to us, to listen attentively to Scripture and what it is saying in the church and in the world.

We need to adopt an internal quiet to wait with and for Jesus. Before his arrest and crucifixion, Jesus taught his disciples how to wait patiently for his return by means of a parable. He taught them to "beware, keep alert; for you do not know when the time will come." This is not an instruction to anxiety, but guidance on attentiveness. The instructions for waiting on Christ are outlined in the parable. The slaves were asked to take charge of the household, "each with his work," and the doorkeeper was commanded "to be on the watch." The household is asked to continue its work and its daily routines with their minds attuned to when the master would return. Jesus calls for vigilance.

In the final part of the image, Jesus instructs his disciples: "Therefore, keep awake—for you do not know when the master of the house will come, in the evening, or at midnight, or at cockcrow, or at dawn, or else he may find you asleep when he comes suddenly. And what I say to you I say to all: Keep awake."

"Keep awake" is not about sleep, but about spiritual torpor, which in our day manifests itself often as busyness in the form of distractedness. Distractedness is a way of not paying attention to oneself or the needs of others or the voice of God because we are so busily doing nothing. Being awake when the Messiah arrives depends upon our ability to wait quietly and to be aware enough to recognize Christ when he comes. To wait for Christ patiently demands active attention. The prophet Isaiah says, "There is no one who calls on your name, / or attempts to take hold of you." But how can one call on someone he or she no longer knows? The difficulty today is not necessarily that people reject Christ, but that they do not know him and so they cannot be awake and attentive to the signs reminding us that the Messiah is coming.

Think about your own busyness and distractedness. How can you focus more fully on the things that matter to you? How can you reduce distractedness as you await the coming of Christ? What needs your full attention today?

THE COMFORT OF HOPE

Second Sunday of Advent

Readings: Isa 40:1-5, 9-11; Ps 85:9-10, 11-12, 13-14;
2 Pet 3:8-14; Mark 1:1-8

"Comfort, O comfort my people, / says your God." (Isa 40:1)

What comfort is there in waiting? Comfort is usually not found standing in line at the DMV or waiting for an appointment at the doctor's office as the minutes tick away. Then you simply hope, as frustration builds, that you can get out as quickly as possible and get on with your life.

This sort of ordinary, everyday hope has to do with desires and wishes that come and go and quickly pass. These everyday hopes can be more significant than this daily drudgery, too, regarding long-term hopes for sports teams, for work, and for family. These are things in which we invest our lives and dream dreams about accomplishments and fulfillment, but these hopes often have to do with "hoping for" something.

But there is another kind of waiting that brings deeper comfort because it is based upon more fundamental hope, a "hoping in" something. Fundamental hope does not have to do with "having" or "acquiring," but is focused on the welfare of people and our hope of salvation. Josef Pieper spoke of fundamental hope as arising when everyday hopes withered and blew away. "Out of the loss of ordinary, everyday hope arises authentic hope," wrote Pieper in *Hope and History* (quoting Herbert Plügge [San Francisco: Ignatius, 1994]). This is the hope of the martyrs, which persists when all human hopes have been vanquished.

This fundamental hope, grounded in the being of the living God of Israel, led Isaiah to call out, "Comfort, O comfort my people, / says your God." What is the comfort that Isaiah is to offer to God's people? It is the promise of God himself, who will act in the future for his people: "See, the Lord God comes with might, / and his arm rules for him; / his reward is with him, / and his recompense before him. / He will feed his flock like a shepherd; / he will gather the lambs in his arms, / and carry them

3

in his bosom, / and gently lead the mother sheep." This promise grounds the fundamental hope of a people who must wait for it in faithfulness. This is hope in the comfort of God.

Isaiah promises that hope will not disappoint, and we are assured in the psalm, "Surely his salvation is at hand for those who fear him, / that his glory may dwell in our land." The Gospel of Mark recalls the words of the prophet Isaiah, seeing the fulfillment of this hope in "the beginning of the good news of Jesus Christ, the Son of God. / As it is written in the prophet Isaiah, / 'See, I am sending my messenger ahead of you, / who will prepare your way; / the voice of one crying out in the wilderness: / "Prepare the way of the Lord, / make his paths straight." ' "

The hope of the early Christians was that Jesus would indeed enact the hopes of Isaiah, establishing the kingdom of never-ending peace and righteousness, the end of waiting in exile banished. When the kingdom was not established in the way the early Christians had hoped, but through the death and resurrection of Jesus Christ, the disciples did not abandon Jesus or his promises but relied upon a more fundamental hope: the truthfulness and faithfulness of God to do what God had promised in a time that is not our own and does not adhere to human schedules or calculations.

In 2 Peter we read "that with the Lord one day is like a thousand years, and a thousand years are like one day. The Lord is not slow about his promise, as some think of slowness, but is patient with you, not wanting any to perish, but all to come to repentance. . . . But, in accordance with his promise, we wait for new heavens and a new earth, where righteousness is at home." This fundamental hope gives us comfort because it is beyond the hopes that disappoint; it is not a "thing" we want or "stuff" we think we need, but the more fundamental reality that gives us deep comfort: Jesus will return and in the returning of Jesus our deepest needs are met. Our waiting is not the absence of hope, or hope dissipating in a dreary waiting room, or dreams that do not come to fruition. It is the comfort of the living God, who comes to us when ordinary hopes disappear and who is coming to us even now. And the joy of this hope gives comfort even in the waiting.

Meditate on the process of waiting in Advent. Do you ever find yourself without hope? How does God's hope come to you? How do you find comfort in hope at Advent?

FULL OF Grace

The Immaculate Conception of the Blessed Virgin Mary

Readings: Gen 3:9-15, 20; Ps 98:1, 2-3, 3-4; Eph 1:3-6, 11-12; Luke 1:26-38

"And he came to her and said, 'Greetings, favored one! The Lord is with you.'" (Luke 1:28)

The feast of the Immaculate Conception developed in the history and life of the church, not simply from Scripture, but from the reflections of the faithful in the church on Mary and her role in salvation history. It was the lived faith of the church that led to the understanding of the immaculate conception of Mary and, secondarily, the writings of theologians reflecting on Scripture and the tradition of the church. These reflections took place over many centuries before being promulgated as a doctrine of the church. The doctrine arose from this lived faith, already accepted within the church by numerous faithful, and contemplation of the requisite holiness necessary for the task to which Mary had been chosen, her sinlessness, and the challenge her sinlessness posed to the doctrine on original sin. In 1854, Pope Pius IX proclaimed, "The most Blessed Virgin Mary was, from the first moment of her conception, by a singular grace and privilege of almighty God and by virtue of the merits of Jesus Christ, Savior of the human race, preserved immune from all stain of original sin" (*Ineffabilis Deus*: DS 2803).

The doctrine of the immaculate conception points to the unique role of Mary in salvation history, and among humanity, but also to the limitations of Scripture without the interpretive and developmental role of tradition and, ultimately, the need for the magisterium of the church as the final interpreter on matters of doctrine.

For the primary teachings of the immaculate conception of Mary are not obviously supported by the biblical passages apart from the interpretive function of the church and the tradition of the church, that which has been revealed to the church through its history, theology, and reflection on the ancient and apostolic tradition. First of all, no passage in the Old or New Testament makes direct reference to Mary's conception. In fact, Mary's conception appears only in a noncanonical text, the Infancy Gospel of James, which is also known as the Protoevangelium of James. In this text, Mary's parents Anna and Joachim are without a child and are given one only after they have offered prayers for a child in light of Anna's barrenness. While the text does not claim Mary is without sin, she is presented as especially pure and as a girl was dedicated as an undefiled virgin to the Jerusalem temple. She remained a virgin, according to the Infancy Gospel of James, even during the birth of Jesus, and perpetually after the birth of Jesus.

While in the past Genesis 3:15 was thought to reference Mary's sinlessness directly, this is no longer thought to be the case. The verse, in the NAB, which is very similar to the NRSV, tells of the enmity between the serpent, the woman, and the woman's offspring: "I will put enmity between you and the woman, / and between your offspring and hers; / He will strike at your head, / while you strike at his heel." The locus for the use of this text in establishing Mary's sinlessness was found in the Vulgate's (mis)translation of "he" for "she": *she* will strike at your head. So, the Douay-Rheims has "I will put enmities between thee and the woman, and thy seed and her seed: she shall crush thy head, and thou shalt lie in wait for her heel." Translators today are of one accord that the reference is to "her offspring," and so the personal pronoun should be translated as "he." Yet, even if the traditional understanding of this passage was maintained, there is no direct claim of Mary's sinlessness.

The key line perhaps in all of Scripture regarding Mary's unique status is in Luke 1:28, in which the Douay-Rheims translates Gabriel's greeting to Mary as "Hail, full of grace, the Lord is with thee." Questions about the traditional rendering of this verse abound, as seen in the NRSV translation, "Greetings, favored one! The Lord is with you." While I think the NRSV translation is weak—does Luke wish to say only that Mary had gained favor?—it raises issues as to how much theological weight should be placed on a simple Greek perfect participle.

The traditional rendering of this perfect participle has understood that Mary had already been graced, that is, the angel Gabriel is acknowledging something about Mary's unique nature. The word "grace" should appear in the translation, but it is still fair to ask, what does "full of grace" mean? It does not clearly indicate on its own, and cannot be pressed to indicate on its own linguistically, that Mary was born free of the stain of original sin.

But it is precisely here where the church—reflecting on the theological reality of Mary expressed by the relevant biblical passages, a significant noncanonical text of the early church, the teachings of the ecumenical council at Ephesus (431) that Mary was the *theotokos*, and the theological developments throughout ecclesiastical history—claims the authority to pronounce on the reality of Mary's sinlessness. The teaching of Mary's immaculate conception developed in the living tradition of the church as it reflected on the holiness necessary for the task to which she had been called and the Scriptures that occasioned this reflection. We should continue to reflect on Mary's holiness, too, for it was through her being prepared to receive the Son of God that the Second Person of the Trinity became incarnate. In order for her to do so it was necessary that she be "full of grace," free from all stain of sin, open to be the handmaiden of the Word so that all the world could encounter the Word in the flesh.

Ponder the unique role and person of Mary. How is she a model of a disciple for you? How does Mary intercede for you with her son, Jesus? As you reflect on these Scriptures, does the role of tradition and the magisterium become more significant for you?

waiTinG on HoPe

Third Sunday of Advent

Readings: Isa 61:1-2a, 10-11; Luke 1:46-48, 49-50, 53-54;
1 Thess 5:16-24; John 1:6-8, 19-28

"Who are you?" (John 1:19)

Christians read the Old Testament today, understandably, in light of Christ's fulfillment of the promises and prophecies found there. It is a simple thing to do, since the early church read the Old Testament in the context of Jesus' incarnation and teaching and the experience of Easter, and then formalized these readings and understandings in the texts of the New Testament.

But what if you were a Jew in the first century, eagerly hoping for the Messiah, a successor to David? These hopes, shared with the whole nation, had been growing since the return from Babylonian exile. As you searched through the panoply of prophecies, you began to wonder, when will these hopes be fulfilled? Who do you look for and where do you start looking? It would be like reading a mystery novel, knowing every clue, studying every sign, but seeing only in retrospect how the whole fits together.

Isaiah 61, for instance, is most often dated to the period just after the return from Babylonian exile, and the author of the passage is generally considered to be the speaker in the text. This prophetic passage emerged, therefore, some five centuries before the birth of Christ. In it the speaker says, "The spirit of the Lord GOD is upon me, / because the LORD has anointed me; / he has sent me to bring good news to the oppressed, / to bind up the brokenhearted, / to proclaim liberty to the captives, / and release to the prisoners." In its original historical context and literal meaning, the author speaks of the conditions that the returning Babylonian exiles found, especially when he promises that those returning exiles "shall build up the ancient ruins, / they shall raise up the former devastations; / they shall repair the ruined cities, / the devastations of many generations." It also seems that the postexilic prophet is speaking of his own role in the restoration of Jerusalem when he says, "The spirit of the Lord God is upon me."

Yet there is also an eschatological edge to the hopes imagined, especially in the proclamation of "the year of the Lord's favor," an event still to come. Christians see the spiritual fulfillment of these proclamations in the person and ministry of Jesus, centuries after they were uttered. The reason is simple: Jesus himself read this passage, according to Luke 4, in the synagogue in Nazareth.

There Jesus says of the Isaian passage, "Today this scripture has been fulfilled in your hearing" (Luke 4:21). This we might identify with what Catholic biblical scholarship has called the *sensus plenior*, or "fuller sense," since it does not obviate the original historical meaning and context but points to a fulfillment of which the original human author was unaware.

This is why the questioning of John the Baptist by some representatives of the Pharisees makes historical and theological sense. The Pharisees, like most Jews of this period, were awaiting the Messiah. Because of the attractiveness of John's prophetic message of repentance to the people, and his popularity, he was someone who had to be examined. They asked, "Who are you?" In response, John confesses that he is not the Messiah, not Elijah, not the prophet and cites Isaiah 40:3, a passage dated to the end of the Babylonian exile: "I am the voice of one crying out in the wilderness, / 'Make straight the way of the Lord.'" John identifies himself not as the Messiah, but as the fulfillment of long-ago prophecies, as the one who prepares the way for the coming Messiah.

But the questions still remained, even for John. Who ever thought that it would happen through a young, unmarried woman, that God would look "with favor on the lowliness of his servant," Mary? God asks that as we wait for fulfillment we be prepared for God to do new things, unexpected things, and be ready for the unlikeliest of answers.

Reflect on the surprises of God's ways. How has God surprised you in the past? How do you wait in hope for the Messiah at Advent? Do you expect God's surprising ways at Advent?

FULFILLMENT OF HOPE

Fourth Sunday of Advent

Readings: 2 Sam 7:1-5, 8b-12, 14a, 16; Ps 89:2-3, 4-5, 27, 29;
Rom 16:25-27; Luke 1:26-38

"Mary said to the angel, 'How can this be, since I am a virgin?'"
(Luke 1:34)

The fulfillment of hope, especially divine hope, fundamental hope, does not rest on intricately calculated human plans, in which we chart the future according to algorithms that never vary and, on the basis of mathematical certainty, await the fulfillment of our calculations. Perhaps this works for 401k plans, but messianic hope is far more significant than investment strategies.

King David had a plan to build God a house (*bēt* in Hebrew), which here indicates the temple. David wanted to build the house of God, and initially the prophet Nathan encouraged him in his plan. But Nathan received the word of the Lord that directed David not to build a *bēt* for God, for God would build David a *bēt*, a dynastic house.

This prophecy seems straightforward when Nathan speaks God's word to David: "I will raise up your offspring after you, who shall come forth from your body, and I will establish his kingdom. He shall build a house for my name, and I will establish the throne of his kingdom forever." Again David is promised, "Your house and your kingdom shall be made sure forever before me; your throne shall be established forever." Is there a question as to what the Davidic kingdom will be?

Such messianic promises are scattered throughout the Old Testament, including Psalm 89, where God says of the king, "I will make him the firstborn, / the highest of the kings of the earth. / Forever I will keep my steadfast love for him, / and my covenant with him will stand firm. / I will establish his line forever, / and his throne as long as the heavens endure." A king forever on the Davidic throne.

We can understand why it was such a crushing blow when the house of David fell with the Babylonian conquest. The house of God was reduced to rubble, the leaders of the people marched into exile, and a king on David's throne was nowhere to be found. When the Persians allowed the Judeans to return to Jerusalem and rebuild the temple, hopes for a restored Davidic kingship began to grow, and they expanded as the king was considered more and more in the light of eschatological and cosmic hopes. God's kingdom would be established as a kingdom to end all kingdoms.

This would not be an ordinary kingdom, but one that drew all nations to it, that foretold a time of peace and prosperity, that would fulfill the hopes and longings of a people bereft of a king for so long. It was their God, of course, the only, true, living God, who would act to establish this kingdom soon. Whenever and however God would do it, its establishment could not be missed.

Unless, of course, the promise was fulfilled through a young virgin, yet to be married, and her infant son, born in the lowliest of circumstances. Mary asks the question, when instructed by the angel Gabriel that she would give birth, "How can this be, since I am a virgin?" It's an excellent question. We might ask other questions, such as, Why do it this way? Why an infant child? Why not a king like David, seated on an earthly throne, attracting all to him with his glory and power?

The angel Gabriel says to Mary, "Do not be afraid, Mary, for you have found favor with God. And now, you will conceive in your womb and bear a son, and you will name him Jesus. He will be great, and will be called the Son of the Most High, and the Lord God will give to him the throne of his ancestor David. He will reign over the house of Jacob forever, and of his kingdom there will be no end."

With Mary and the Jews at Jesus' time, we might say that we did not see this coming. But as Gabriel says of Elizabeth's pregnancy, "nothing will be impossible with God." And Mary's final response is calm acceptance: "let it be with me according to your word."

As we reflect on how God has confounded human expectations in the past, only to fulfill these hopes more majestically than we could imagine, we need these words on our lips at Christmas: "nothing will be impossible with God." However God will do it, be ready, for God fulfills hope in ways never before imagined. We need to be able to say with Mary, "let it be with me according to your word."

Visualize Mary with the angel. Are you open to God speaking to you? Are you ready to say yes to God? How does the past fulfillment of God's promises guide you to hope at Advent?

GOD AMONG US

The Nativity of the Lord

Readings: Isa 52:7-10; Ps 98:1, 2-3, 3-4, 5-6;
Heb 1:1-6; John 1:1-18

"He is the reflection of God's glory and the exact imprint of God's very being." (Heb 1:3)

Do we take the incarnation for granted? Do we read biblical passages that tell us that Christ "sustains all things by his powerful word" and give a shrug, if only an intellectual or spiritual shrug? Have we truly considered and wondered that God, through whom "all things came into being . . . and without him not one thing came into being," was born to a woman and lived among us? I ask these questions because when I do contemplate that "the Word became flesh and lived among us," and not simply muse about it as a mundane reality, it is breathtaking in its beauty. Perhaps even more than breathtaking, it is mind-boggling.

In trying to understand God, as we should, or taking God for granted, as we should not, we sometimes diminish or forget God's majesty. This is why the prologue of John's gospel reminds us of the creation narratives in Genesis. The gospel tells us that God is the creator of all things, but also before all things, and that Christ, the Word, was with God bringing all things into being. The incarnation is not about cutting God down to a manageable size or diminishing God's majesty; it is a sign of God's love for all humanity.

The incarnation itself, apart from Jesus' salvific action on the cross and through the resurrection, is itself a sign of God's desire to be with us. Saint Thomas Aquinas, writing in the *Summa Theologica* 3.1.2, says that "human beings who are seen are not to be followed; God who cannot be seen is to be followed; therefore, that who is to be seen and who is to be followed could be one person, God became a human being." But not only does this give us our model to follow, God in the flesh, it shows to us our divine destiny and displays the great dignity of human nature.

This is the sign of God's love for humanity because God did not have to do it this way. God did it this way for us. "God was not obliged to save mankind in this way, but human nature needed to make amends to God like this" (St. Anselm, *Meditation on Human Redemption*). To restore human nature it was necessary that someone who was like us in every way could pay a debt that we could not. Human nature alone could not do this, but the debt had to be paid. While God could simply just ignore human sin, in what way would that grant human freedom, dignity, or goodness?

So the goodness of God came to help and the Son of God assumed manhood in his own person so that God and man should be one person, one and the same person. This life of God made man, who came to us as an infant, brought into the world more goodness than the weight of all human sins are bad. As the author of the Letter to the Hebrews writes, Christ, "when he had made purification for sins, he sat down at the right hand of the Majesty on high, having become as much superior to angels as the name he has inherited is more excellent than theirs." This was the ultimate purpose of the incarnation: to save us from our sins.

Yet, God became our exemplar and model by sharing in human life, not for a moment, not simply for the purposes of making purification for our sins, or exhibiting might and majesty, but to take on the whole human experience. God became man and shared in human life, as an infant, a child, a teenager, and a man; loved by his mother and father; surrounded by family and friends and celebrating life with them, festivals in Jerusalem and Shabbat dinners in Nazareth and Capernaum. He went to synagogue, walked down dusty Galilean roads, talked with his friends, and broiled fish at the seaside over a charcoal fire.

He came to earth as a vulnerable infant to teach us how to live together and to love together. And God did this all out of love for us, which seems to me a great reason to celebrate Christmas. We celebrate the redemption of the human race the infant Jesus brought with him, so long ago in a manger, his mother and father gathered around him; but shepherds, wise men, animals, all there too. The goodness of human life, the promise of eternal life soon to be fulfilled. Yet, in the incarnation, a babe in a humble manger, no place in the inn for the Son of God come to earth, God was not diminished or humbled, but human nature was exalted. God was not made any less, but humankind was mercifully helped for all eternity when the infant Jesus was born.

Contemplate the incarnation of God, who took on human flesh and lived among us. How does Jesus' incarnation help you understand God's love for us? How does the birth of the infant Christ demonstrate God's willingness to share in our sorrows and needs? How does God's humility in coming to live among us reflect on God's majesty and power?

CHILDren OF HOPe

The Holy Family of Jesus, Mary, and Joseph

Readings: Gen 15:1-6; 21:1-3; Ps 105:1-2, 3-4, 6-7, 8-9;
Heb 11:8, 11-12, 17-19; Luke 2:22-40

*"And the child's father and mother were amazed at
what was being said about him."* (Luke 2:33)

The truth of the supposedly clichéd phrase "every child is a miracle"
hits home for most people when a child is born to them or an adopted
child is welcomed into the family. The instantaneous recognition of the
child never before seen is a spiritual experience made tactile as a mother
takes the newborn in her arms and a father gazes at an infant who evokes
on sight the deepest of loves.

We tend to think of childbirth, especially today, as something that is
simple and straightforward. It is certainly natural; and for many people,
both in conception and at delivery, it poses no problems. Yet, there are
many others for whom having a child is a struggle. We have no idea why
some couples have no children and other families have one, why some
women have miscarried numerous times or had ectopic pregnancies that
threaten the lives of mother and child. We should never judge the size of
a family, for we have no knowledge of the hidden burdens that many
women and men carry. Many of the model families throughout the Bible
were overjoyed that God blessed them with one child, a child they had
long desired.

The miraculous nature of conception and childbirth is a theme that
runs through the Old Testament and is often seen in families that have
only one child. Numerous women who were considered "barren" give
birth to a child of hope, often when it seemed such hope was out of reach.
In this number we count Rebekah, Hannah, and the mother of Samson,
all blessed with children when it seemed it could never happen. But the
preeminent example is the first one we see in Genesis: Sarah.

Sarah was too old, as was Abram, to have and raise a child. Genesis
tells us she was ninety years old and Abram one hundred. Abram peti-

tioned God, saying, "You have given me no offspring, and so a slave born in my house is to be my heir." God promises Abram, "This man shall not be your heir; no one but your very own issue shall be your heir." But how could it be? Sarah laughed at the promise of a child given to her after natural hope had vanished.

But God gave them Isaac, a child of promise and hope for Abram, now called Abraham, and Sarah and for the future of a promised nation. The promised Messiah would come from this lineage and be given miraculously to Mary, which reveals another part of the equation: never having engaged in sexual intercourse, she was given a child by God—a child given to this new mother and her husband-to-be, but a child of hope for the whole world.

Yet the stories of the matriarchs, Mary, and their unique children indicate to us the miraculous nature of every birth. True, our children will probably not be patriarchs of a nation, as Isaac was for Israel; and certainly none can be Jesus, the Messiah, the Savior, both God and man. But the mothers were real mothers, just like women today, who raise many children or one child, or yearn for a child. And their children were real children, who had to be loved and raised. God chose to work his miracles not in opposition to nature but through the most natural of ways: childbirth.

But every family, whether gifted with many children or none or one, has a role to play in God's dramatic story of salvation and shares in the miraculous gift of hope children represent. Each child has been willed by God to serve a unique purpose.

And it was through the birth of one child that all of us share in the hope of salvation. As Simeon says in Luke's gospel of the newborn baby boy Jesus, "My eyes have seen your salvation, / which you have prepared in the presence of all peoples, / a light for revelation to the Gentiles / and for glory to your people Israel."

Mary and Joseph were "amazed at what was being said about him," for he was the fulfillment of all hopes. But in the reality of the Holy Family, we see the miraculous nature of every child and every family reflected.

Consider the joys and sorrows of family life. How has God blessed your family? How has God acted in your family, both now and in the past? How does the Holy Family inspire your family in hope?

THE MOTHER OF JESUS

*"So they went with haste and found Mary and Joseph,
and the child lying in the manger."* (Luke 2:16)

Why do we call Mary the mother of God? It might be because the Council of Ephesus, in AD 431, declared her to be *theotokos*, literally "the bearer of God," or that her cousin Elizabeth exclaimed when Mary visited her, "And why has this happened to me, that the mother of my Lord comes to me?" (Luke 1:43). Both of these, the statement of an ecumenical council and the biblical passage, indicate that Mary is the mother of a divine figure, *theos* (God) and *kyrios* (Lord), which indeed she is, but she is also the mother of a human being, infant, boy, teenager, man, Jesus of Nazareth, born in Bethlehem of Judea, whom she nursed and raised. She is the mother of God, mother of Jesus.

Mary was chosen from among all women to bear the Son of God and to be the *theotokos* she had been chosen and prepared, "full of grace": "from the first instant of her conception, she was totally preserved from the stain of original sin and she remained pure from all personal sin throughout her life" (*Catechism of the Catholic Church*, 2nd ed. [United States Catholic Conference—Libreria Editrice Vaticana, 1997], 508). Jesus was conceived by the Holy Spirit and Mary remained a virgin throughout her life, which is why the church has declared her "perpetually virgin." According to the Vatican II document *Lumen Gentium* (56), Mary is seen "not merely as a passive instrument in the hands of God, but as freely cooperating in the work of human salvation through faith and obedience" (Austin Flannery, ed., *Vatican Council II: Constitutions, Decrees, Declarations; The Basic Sixteen Documents* [Collegeville, MN: Liturgical Press, 2014]). It is Mary's free cooperation that led to church fathers to define her as "the Mother of the living" and the new Eve, who brings life to a world in the clutches of death through her son Jesus. As the apostle Paul said, "God sent his Son, born of a woman, born under the law, in order to redeem those who were under the law, so that we might receive adoption as children" (Gal 4:4-5).

For this we needed the Son, but for the Son, we needed the mother. Again, *Lumen Gentium* 60–62 is quick to acknowledge that the role of Mary is not the equal of her son, but "she conceived, gave birth to, and nourished Christ, she presented him to the Father in the temple, shared his sufferings as he died on the Cross" (61). Because of the concreteness of God's incarnation, fully human, a son among family and friends, a mother was necessary to raise the child and aid in his human development. Her work was not done when she said yes to God that she carry the Son of God or give birth to the miraculous child; a mother's work was just beginning, as she would nurse and swaddle the infant and after eight days take him to the temple to be circumcised according to the law of Moses for every Jewish boy. This is what makes her the mother of Jesus: the daily work of being a mother in response to God's call to her.

This is also what makes the mother of Jesus, the mother of God, an archetype for every follower of her son. She is the first disciple of Jesus, the model for every Christian, united to her son and his mission with complete loyalty and humility. In what must have been the most difficult moment of her life, she was at the foot of the cross when he died. Mary bore witness to Jesus' life, but also to his death. It is important to see the reality of this event because it seems that nothing could be harder than to witness not just the death of one's son, but the unjust cruelty that preceded it and the unjust verdict that allowed it to take place. This is where her "yes," given to the birth of her infant son, was transformed into the "yes" that led to his painful death, but that allowed him to secure redemption for humanity. In the Gospel of John 19:26, Jesus says to his mother, "Woman, here is your son."

Naturally, or supernaturally, she continued to remain faithful to the church and its work even after her son's death, as Acts 1:14 tells us that the apostles and some others, "including Mary the mother of Jesus," "were constantly devoting themselves to prayer." "By her complete adherence to the Father's will, to his Son's redemptive work, and to every prompting of the Holy Spirit, the Virgin Mary is the church's model of faith and charity. Thus she is a 'preeminent and . . . wholly unique member of the Church'; indeed, she is the 'exemplary realization' (*typus*) of the Church" (*Catechism of the Catholic Church*, 967).

Mary, in a profound sense, though given a unique role in salvation history and a unique end to her life to bring her to heavenly glory, shows through the mundane work of a mother her constant obedience to God's will. Her will was devoted to God and God's kingdom, a journey all of us are called to take and the goal for which all of us strive. She shares already the destiny for which all of us are intended—that of the paradise of heaven—and her faithfulness opened the door for her son to complete his mission. By being his mother, she also opens the door "so that we might receive adoption as children." Mother of Jesus, mother of God, mother to all of us.

Reflect on Mary as mother of God, mother of Jesus. How has she become a model for your Christian life? In what way do you look to her for guidance? Do you see her as a mother to you?

Journey of Hope

The Epiphany of the Lord

Readings: Isa 60:1-6; Ps 72:1-2, 7-8, 10-11, 12-13;
Eph 3:2-3a, 5-6; Matt 2:1-12

"Where is the child who has been born king of the Jews?" (Matt 2:2)

A summer ago my family set off on a cross-country car trip from Minnesota to Vancouver, BC, in part to pick up a wooden bench that my great-grandfather had made when my family immigrated to Canada. It was the first thing he built when he arrived. As an old man, he was too old to work in the fields, so he took care of his grandchildren as they played outside and he needed a bench to sit on.

About two hours into our journey, we realized that we had forgotten our passports. We had to turn around and drive back home, which added four hours to our long and looming drive time. It was an unforeseen glitch, and all journeys are full of them. But when there is a purpose to your journey, all the missteps are made worthwhile.

On the porch of my house an old bench sits now, almost ninety years old. It is not much of a bench in some ways. It is a simple bench, built without screws or nails. It is a connection to our family's past, a journey of hope for our future. We drove a long way to bring it home.

According to the Gospel of Matthew, the magi knew where they were traveling and they knew whom they had come to see, for they asked, "Where is the child who has been born king of the Jews? For we observed his star at its rising, and have come to pay him homage." The late Raymond E. Brown, SS, reminds us that beyond the historical realities of their journey are deeper spiritual realities that Matthew's gospel is driving at, connecting the natural revelation of the pagan world to the revelation of the Jewish Scripture and to the divine manifestation of Jesus himself.

But when we imagine the journey, coming from ancient Persia, Babylon, or Arabia, we wonder, what had they experienced to arrive in Bethlehem? How long was a journey of hundreds of miles on camel, donkey, or foot?

Did they ever think to turn around and just go home? Matthew does not focus on their daunting journey, however, only on their arrival, because they had traveled to discover the source of salvation.

But when they arrived, they were lacking something, which is why they went to Herod. What they lacked was the special revelation given to the Jews, as embodied in Matthew's citation, combined from Micah 5:1 and 2 Samuel 5:2: "And you, Bethlehem, in the land of Judah, / are by no means least among the rulers of Judah; / for from you shall come a ruler / who is to shepherd my people Israel."

As for the magi, "When they saw that the star had stopped, they were overwhelmed with joy. On entering the house, they saw the child with Mary his mother; and they knelt down and paid him homage. Then, opening their treasure chests, they offered him gifts of gold, frankincense, and myrrh." On a journey of hope, the disappointments and struggles dissipate the moment you arrive at your destination.

They would return home warily because they had been "warned in a dream not to return to Herod," but it is not wrong to suspect that they were transformed people when they arrived back home, for they brought home a new light. Compare this to Herod, who had access to the revelation of Scripture but whose only journey was one of despair. Jesus was a threat to Herod's narrowly conceived power; the hope represented by Jesus was something to destroy, not celebrate.

Perhaps the magi faced questions when they returned about why they traveled so far: Why go to see this child? Why follow that star? It was a journey of hope, not just for them, but for all of humanity. Father Brown went on to say of this journey, "In these Magi Matthew sees an anticipation of Jesus' promise, 'I tell you, many will come from east and west and will eat with Abraham and Isaac and Jacob in the kingdom of heaven' (8:11)" (*The Birth of the Messiah* [New Haven, CT: Yale, 1999]). The magi, ultimately, are a symbol of the journey we are all on, the true journey, which takes us not far from home, but back home to God. This God took on human form and came to us as an infant child to show us how to journey home.

Contemplate your own journey. Have you ever wondered about the path you were taking? Have you sought guidance from Scripture? How does God coming to live among us help you on your journey?

SPIRIT OF JUSTICE

"I have baptized you with water;
but he will baptize you with the Holy Spirit." (Mark 1:8)

In a number of Servant Songs in Isaiah, a mysterious individual appears who sometimes represents the nation of Israel, though later Christians understood him to represent Jesus. In Isaiah 42, this person is designated "my servant" (*ʿebed* in Hebrew), while in the Septuagint "my child" (*pais* in Greek) is identified with the nation of Israel. But whether we see the servant, God's child, as the nation of Israel or as a prefiguring of Jesus Christ, God's son, the task remains the same: the servant is called to bring forth justice. Isaiah writes, "a bruised reed he will not break, / and a dimly burning wick he will not quench; / he will faithfully bring forth justice." Justice will be served, but with meekness and gentleness.

The servant has been consecrated for this job "as a covenant to the people, / a light to the nations, / to open the eyes that are blind, / to bring out the prisoners from the dungeon, / from the prison those who sit in darkness." In times of social travail, as now in the United States—which imprisons a greater percentage of its people than any other country, in which the not yet healed scars of slavery and injustice are reopened by ongoing racism and injustice, and in which police officers meant to serve and protect fellow citizens are sometimes seen as oppressors of their brothers and sisters—the servant's Spirit-filled demand for justice resonates anew.

Mark and the other gospels point to Jesus' baptism as the starting point for the Spirit-empowered work of the servant, God's son. The Spirit descended "like a dove on him," but John the Baptist's words indicate that Jesus' baptism was only the beginning of the Spirit's work. As John the Baptist says to his disciples, "I have baptized you with water; but he will

23

baptize you with the Holy Spirit." Jesus was baptized as a model for his disciples, the men and women who make up the church, to follow in his footsteps, to share not just in the repentance that the water represented but also in the outpouring of the Holy Spirit that Jesus brought.

The Acts of the Apostles makes clear that the Spirit descending upon Jesus at his baptism was the model for the outpouring of the Spirit upon the whole church. Peter tells us that this message of repentance and justice began "in Galilee after the baptism that John announced: how God anointed Jesus of Nazareth with the Holy Spirit and with power." The church was then empowered to carry on and continue the work of the servant Jesus Christ. The church was emboldened to embody justice and light for all people. Peter's speech, in which he tells his hearers that "in every nation anyone who fears him and does what is right is acceptable" to God, follows the baptism of Cornelius and his family.

Who is Cornelius? Only a Roman centurion, a symbol of the oppressive military power of the Roman Empire that had subjugated the Jewish state for a century. Yet Cornelius's conversion tells us that the Spirit can and will convert any heart. For even though we, as human beings and as Christians, sometimes embody partiality, God shows no partiality. God's son came to identify with each of us, regardless of race, ability, challenges, or sins. God knows us all and loves us all. God loves Tamir Rice, Michael Brown, and Eric Garner, just as God loves Cornelius, the centurion, and as God loves the police officers, those who act for justice and those who break the hope of justice.

Christ's baptism creates for us the beginning of a paradigm upon which we model our lives after the Just One. Just as Christ invites us to baptism, in order to participate in justice, we need to offer the invitation to God's table, so that people know that God's hospitality welcomes all. The promise of the just Son of God, the one who is for all people, makes us yearn for him, but also emboldens us to act for justice now, as we have the model to emulate. We need to yearn for the Spirit to move us to repentance, to challenge our prejudices and sins, rooted so deeply in our hearts, to ask how we can change not only unjust societies and institutions, but our own hearts.

Reflect on a current instance of injustice. Can you invite the Spirit to transform the sinfulness in your life and the sinfulness in our society? How can you act to heal injustice and sin in your own life and in society?

In THe WILDerness

First Sunday of Lent

Readings: Gen 9:8-15; Ps 25:4-5, 6-7, 8-9;
1 Pet 3:18-22; Mark 1:12-15

"Repent, and believe in the good news." (Mark 1:15)

Many theological reasons for Jesus' baptism have been proposed, explaining it as a sacramental model for the church, an act of solidarity with sinful humanity, or "a manifestation of his self-emptying" (*Catechism of the Catholic Church*, 1224), but any answer must stress that "the baptism of Jesus is on his part the acceptance and inauguration of his mission as God's suffering Servant. He allows himself to be numbered among sinners" (CCC 536). After Jesus' baptism, "the Spirit immediately drove him out into the wilderness." Because Jesus aligns himself with sinful humanity, the act immediately following his baptism is to do battle with evil, as each of us must do daily.

Jesus, who takes on all of our humanity, did not travel from baptism straight to the glory of the transfiguration but went from baptism to the wilderness, because it is a place that haunts our fragile humanity no matter where we are, and it demands redemption. Jesus' redemption of humanity begins with the incarnation, but we see it advance in his obedience (unlike Adam and Eve) to the will of God and in his steadfastness to resist temptation.

The model Jesus presents to us when "he was in the wilderness forty days, tempted by Satan" is one grounded in the reality of human life. Life can be hard, life can be unfair, and life can knock you to the ground. A promise to relax in the car on the way to work can deteriorate into curses cast against the first driver to cut you off. A promise not to drink, and all the hard work that accompanied it in rehab, can fall apart in one visit to the bar, resulting in a sense of frustration and ineptitude. A family gathered in joy can be smashed apart with the sudden death of a child, plunging people into suffering and darkness. Sin crouches nearby, to tempt us in our struggles, our losses, and our suffering.

Unlike Jesus, our ability to resist temptation is flawed, even with the gift of baptism, but baptism also allows us to seek safety in the church when evil threatens to overcome us and drive us into the wilderness alone. For Jesus comes out of the wilderness proclaiming, "The time is fulfilled, and the kingdom of God has come near; repent, and believe in the good news." The church was built for the ongoing battle and for repentance when we fall. Repentance is a sign of why the church was built: for salvation.

Noah's ark was built to save those who took refuge in it, and God promised that "the waters shall never again become a flood to destroy all flesh." This ark is an ancient Christian image for the church, for as it says in 1 Peter, by it "a few, that is, eight persons, were saved through water"; but in a spiritual sense "baptism, which this prefigured, now saves you— not as a removal of dirt from the body, but as an appeal to God for a good conscience, through the resurrection of Jesus Christ." Repentance functions as this "appeal to God for a good conscience."

Repentance is available to us because Jesus chose to align himself in the battle against evil so fully that after emerging from the wilderness, "Christ also suffered for sins once for all, the righteous for the unrighteous, in order to bring you to God. He was put to death in the flesh, but made alive in the spirit, in which also he went and made a proclamation to the spirits in prison, who in former times did not obey, when God waited patiently in the days of Noah, during the building of the ark." There is a question as to whom these "spirits in prison" represent—whether these spirits are the "fallen angels" or the human dead of the time of Noah—but Jesus' proclamation to them is built into the church for us: "Repent, and believe in the good news"!

It is Christ—through his battle with evil in the wilderness, his suffering and death, and finally his resurrection—who has gained salvation for us. Christ, who is raised up and at the right hand of God, has authority over all powers, human and demonic. We must be encouraged to fearlessly grasp our baptismal mission, for there is no power over which Christ does not rule, and that mission includes repentance when we stumble in our own personal battles.

Let Jesus be with you in the wilderness. What temptations are you struggling with today? For what do you need to repent? How has God accompanied you in your times in the wilderness?

Hearing God Speak

Second Sunday of Lent

Readings: Gen 22:1-2, 9a, 10-13, 15-18; Ps 116:10, 15, 16-17, 18-19;
Rom 8:31b-34; Mark 9:2-10

"This is my Son, the Beloved; listen to him!" (Mark 9:7)

The first thing Abraham had to do was listen to God, but Abraham also had to be willing to hear God, no matter the word spoken. And the word Abraham first heard from God, the command to sacrifice his beloved son Isaac, remains even now at some level inconceivable and incomprehensible. Why would God ask Abraham to kill the child in whom the divine promises of Israel were embedded?

Yes, we know from the text of Genesis that it was a test. Abraham heard the voice of God and an outrageous request, yet the patriarch trusted God. This was a test for Abraham, not God, for God knew Abraham would obey, but Abraham's willingness to listen would reveal the true nature of God.

The voice of God that Abraham heard was true both times. If Abraham had not heeded the voice of God initially, would he have realized that God had truly spoken a second time, when he told Abraham not to sacrifice his son Isaac? What if Abraham had listened to the first voice alone and rejected God's directive to spare Isaac? Not only would Isaac have died, but the true nature of God would not have been revealed. There is no question that the mystery and unknowability of God are wrapped up in the narrative, but this challenging narrative demonstrates Abraham's willingness always to be attentive and obedient to God's will.

We do not know how fearful Isaac was or if he understood what was taking place. Ancient and medieval Jewish commentators like Philo, Josephus, and Rashi proposed that he might have been seven or twenty-five or even thirty-seven years old when the Akedah took place—but when Isaac calls out "Father!" and asks where the lamb is for the burnt offering, Abraham remains faithful, saying, "God himself will provide the lamb for a burnt offering, my son."

Abraham's faithfulness rained down God's blessings on him, for God said to Abraham, "Because you have done this, and have not withheld your son, your only son, I will indeed bless you." Yet Abraham's obedient listening had an impact far beyond his own family and people, for he was also promised that "by your offspring shall all the nations of the earth gain blessing for themselves, because you have obeyed my voice."

Jesus, too, always heard the voice of God the Father and remained obedient to it. For Jesus, the threat of sacrifice went beyond Isaac's questioning to the reality of Calvary, yet Jesus trusted that God, "who did not withhold his own Son, but gave him up for all of us," will always, as Paul says, be "for us."

Still, when Jesus in the Gospel of Mark told his apostles that he must suffer and die, Peter rejected Jesus' word outright, even though Jesus' narrative of suffering concluded with the resurrection. Peter and the other apostles rejected God's way of suffering and sought the glory that they knew was the essence of God. And it was. For "six days later, Jesus took with him Peter and James and John, and led them up a high mountain apart, by themselves. And he was transfigured before them, and his clothes became dazzling white, such as no one on earth could bleach them." These chosen apostles stood in the midst of glory, terrified, and heard, like Abraham, the voice of God: "This is my Son, the Beloved; listen to him!"

But the God who showed them a vision of heavenly glory and spoke to them out of the glory was the same God who spoke to them when Jesus said that he would suffer and die. When you listen to God, you do not get to pick just the "good stuff," the words that appeal to you: God asks that you listen always.

But trials, tests, and suffering are not the end of the story. Paul asks us in Romans, "What then are we to say about these things? If God is for us, who is against us? He who did not withhold his own Son, but gave him up for all of us, will he not with him also give us everything else?" The end of the story is God's glory, but it requires hearing God's voice in the midst of trials, suffering, pain, and loss, even when it seems to be God's voice commanding the suffering. Be patient and listen again, for the voice of God desires only our blessing.

Ponder the times you have listened for God's voice. When have you heard it? Where do you hear it most clearly? In Scripture, among your friends, in church? What do you hear God saying to you?

GOD'S WORD FOR US

Third Sunday of Lent

Readings: Exod 20:1-17; Ps 19:8, 9, 10, 11;
1 Cor 1:22-25; John 2:13-25

"Stop making my Father's house a marketplace!" (John 2:16)

There is no question about the centrality of the Ten Commandments to Judaism and subsequently to Christianity. The Ten Words, as the Old Testament itself calls them (Exod 34:28; Deut 4:13), or Decalogue, which God spoke to Moses, resonate down through the centuries into our lives. The *Catechism of the Catholic Church* (2056–63), however, stresses not just the importance of the commandments but their embeddedness in the lives of the people of Israel.

These words God spoke come in the context of the exodus story and in the covenant God made with Israel. As a result, the Catechism claims that the commandments "properly so-called come in the second place: they express the implications of belonging to God through the establishment of the covenant. Moral existence is a *response* to the Lord's loving initiative" (2062).

Waldemar Janzen speaks of the Ten Commandments and the other collections of laws found in the Old Testament as examples of God's ways, saying, "The positive laws in their smaller or larger collections offer samples pointing to an integrated value system, an ethos, that lies behind them and that generated them" (*Old Testament Ethics* [Louisville, KY: Westminster John Knox, 1994], 88). The Ten Words are not the end of moral obligations but the beginning of a life in response to the complete call to love God and to love our neighbor.

It is this deep desire to help us see beyond laws as the rote fulfillment of commands, as check marks to tick off—a temptation all of us face in our religious lives—that drives Jesus in the gospel story most often referred to as the cleansing of the temple.

There were laws governing the temple's operations and the sacrificial system, and these laws also were revealed by God, but in the practice of them Jesus perceives something lacking. So "he told those who were selling the doves, 'Take these things out of here! Stop making my Father's house a marketplace!' His disciples remembered that it was written, 'Zeal for your house will consume me.' " It is this zeal for God's house that motivates Jesus and ought to push us to look beyond the surface events.

For it is not obvious what precisely is wrong with buying and selling animals for sacrifice or with exchanging money for pilgrims who have traveled from far-away countries and need to pay the half shekel temple tax (Exod 30:11-16), but at the Passover that year Jesus "found people selling cattle, sheep, and doves, and the money changers seated at their tables. Making a whip of cords, he drove all of them out of the temple, both the sheep and the cattle. He also poured out the coins of the money changers and overturned their tables." The Passover celebrates the exodus, that time when the Ten Words were given by God to Moses to pass on to the Israelites wandering in the wilderness. The celebration of Passover looks to the past and to the future of salvation, and Jesus found the response to God's salvation wanting.

What was lacking? This is a question difficult to answer. Was it simply the buying and selling that seemed incongruent in God's temple? Or is Jesus pointing us to the depths of salvation? Janzen says that "the grandeur and centrality of the Decalogue within the canonical story . . . remains uncontested. This code stands at the head of all subsequent legislation gathered under the name of Moses and, in a sense, comprehends the purpose of that legislation. It is God's call to Israel to respond to salvation with a new way of life. This new life can be summarized elsewhere as a total commitment to love (Deut 6:45)" (ibid., 89). Did Jesus see the total commitment to love lacking?

What if we imagine Jesus cleansing our own lives, challenging our regular way of business, our claims that we are following all the rules and doing what the commandments say? Would Jesus push us beyond the rules or the way things are done? The rules, his actions say, while essential, are not the end of the story. God calls us to a deeper commitment, to a purification of our lives, which calls on us to make central not commandments but the reality of God who spoke those commandments. Jesus asks us to shape our lives in conformity with love, for "moral existence is a response to the Lord's loving initiative."

Picture Jesus in the temple; now picture him in your life. How is Jesus challenging you to change? How is he cleansing your life? Is he challenging your regular way of business?

THe weakness OF SIN

Fourth Sunday of Lent

Readings: 2 Chr 36:14-16, 19-23; Ps 137:1-2, 3, 4-5, 6;
Eph 2:4-10; John 3:14-21

*"Indeed, God did not send the Son into the world
to condemn the world."* (John 3:17)

One of the darkest times in the life of the Jewish people was the destruction of Jerusalem and the temple by the Babylonians and the subsequent exile of the people of God. According to the Chronicler, this was not an action God wanted, "but they kept mocking the messengers of God, despising his words, and scoffing at his prophets, until the wrath of the LORD against his people became so great that there was no remedy." Only then did the Babylonians come.

And the Babylonians came with fury. They killed young and old alike "and had no compassion on young man or young woman, the aged or the feeble"; the wealth of the king was looted and brought to Babylon; the temple was burned to the ground and the walls of Jerusalem broken down; and those who were not killed were taken into exile in Babylon to become servants.

It was as they were weeping by the rivers of Babylon that God came to the exiled Jews and told them to go home. This return was brought about by the conquerors of Babylon, King Cyrus of Persia and his army, "in fulfillment of the word of the LORD spoken by Jeremiah." Out of the darkness came light.

It was not the case that God's salvation came because the lives of the Judeans were now lived in perfect righteousness, but because God looked with mercy upon his people. We know from Ezra, Nehemiah, and Haggai that the people needed to return to the forgotten law of God, reform their lives, and rebuild the ruined temple. God did not wait for them to achieve righteousness but allowed the conditions for righteousness to flourish.

This is precisely the point made by the author of the Letter to the Ephesians, traditionally thought to be Paul, who speaks of God reaching out to humanity "even when we were dead through our trespasses." God reached out to reward us not because we had achieved the necessary level of righteousness but because God is merciful and desires to seat us "in the heavenly places in Christ Jesus, so that in the ages to come he might show the immeasurable riches of his grace in kindness toward us in Christ Jesus." This all takes place through God's gracious initiative.

Ephesians says that "by grace you have been saved through faith, and this is not your own doing; it is the gift of God." This could not be clearer: salvation is gift, salvation is grace. Yet we are also told that we are saved "through faith" (*pistis*), which is itself a part of the gift. Salvation cannot be earned, bought, or bargained for, but faith is the essential human response. Faith in God's gracious gift allows us to be conformed to God's image, since we were "created in Christ Jesus for good works [*ergois agathois*], which God prepared beforehand to be our way of life."

In John's gospel Jesus tells us that "God so loved the world that he gave his only Son, so that everyone who believes in him may not perish but may have eternal life." The word translated "believe" in John 3:16 is the verbal form of *pistis*, the same word translated "faith" in Ephesians. All who have faith (*pisteuōn*) in God's Son are on the path to conforming themselves to God's image in order to share in eternal life or, in the language of Ephesians, to share Christ's life in "the heavenly places."

It is this faith that allows us, even in our sinful state, to see that the "light has come into the world" and "those who do what is true come to the light, so that it may be clearly seen that their deeds [*erga*] have been done in God." Ephesians tells us that we have been created for "good works," while the Gospel of John says those in the "light" do their "deeds" in God. The same Greek word (*ergon*) lies behind "works" in Ephesians and "deeds" in the Gospel of John.

God's salvation is an undeserved gift that begins with faith. But our response to God's grace naturally blossoms into good works, "so that it may be clearly seen that their deeds have been done in God." These deeds are not the means to merit salvation but the joyous response to God's merciful gift of salvation and the path to grow in holiness and closeness to God.

Reflect on God's gracious gift. How has your faith grown over the years? How has God's gift inspired you to good works? Are you taking joy in following God?

FOLLOWING THE SERVANT

Fifth Sunday of Lent

Readings: Jer 31:31-34; Ps 51:3-4, 12-13, 14-15;
Heb 5:7-9; John 12:20-33

"Whoever serves me must follow me, and where I am,
there will my servant be also." (John 12:26)

When we hear of the martyrdom of Christians, like the twenty-one Coptic Christians killed in Libya on February 15, 2015, we identify with them immediately as disciples of Jesus and as our brothers and sisters in Christ. However little we might know about the history of the Coptic Christians, in their suffering witness we recognize them as family, servants of Christ. Martyrdom purges the ephemera of human life to reveal its cruciform meaning.

We recognize in their suffering the witness and model of Jesus. It is through sharing in our human suffering that Jesus is able to sympathize with us. The Letter to the Hebrews tells us that "in the days of his flesh, Jesus offered up prayers and supplications, with loud cries and tears, to the one who was able to save him from death," desirous, as we all are, to avoid suffering if possible.

Yet the Gospel of John explains that when Jesus acknowledged "my soul is troubled" as he waited on the cusp of suffering, he also asked, "And what should I say—'Father, save me from this hour'?" For our sake, Jesus remained a servant to the will of the Father and offered a yes to his destiny because "it is for this reason that I have come to this hour."

What was this reason? "Unless a grain of wheat falls into the earth and dies, it remains just a single grain; but if it dies, it bears much fruit." What Jesus' death offers, unlike any other death, is the possibility of salvation for humanity. Through his death, Jesus offers to us the model of the faithful witness, but more than that the model witness is the source of salvation. The path of Jesus, Hebrews says, was the process through which "he learned obedience through what he suffered; and having been made perfect, he became the source of eternal salvation for all who obey him."

This is why Jesus warns that "those who love their life lose it," for the gains and power of this world can entrap and distract us from the weight of discipleship. Instead, "whoever serves me must follow me, and where I am, there will my servant be also." Discipleship might indeed entail suffering and loss now, but whoever follows Jesus is tracking the path he has cleared to eternal life. For all who face suffering, as Jesus did, the desire to be saved from suffering is profoundly human. Nevertheless, the humanity of Jesus is real and the choice he made on our behalf was freely chosen.

And yet a most profound difference exists between us and our model Jesus: sin. We have it; Jesus did not. This is why our prayers and supplications are offered to God in the key of repentance. Repentance emerges when we recognize the suffering we create when we sin and the broken relationship with God sin produces. When we cry out to God our sincere desire that we might turn from sin, we echo the plea in today's psalm: "Create in me a clean heart, O God, / and put a new and right spirit within me." We have constant need to renew ourselves along the path of discipleship.

We have a means of salvation and through Jesus the means also to repent when we fall away from it. Through confession, prayer, fasting, almsgiving, and all the other spiritual and corporal works of mercy, we can seek to have God's law before us at all times, inscribed on our hearts. We can seek to have our most crooked hearts straightened again by the love and mercy of God.

And even more, by shaping our lives in the model of Jesus, even when it entails the possibility of suffering that might lead even to death, we can become models for others. As the psalmist calls out, "Restore to me the joy of your salvation, / and sustain in me a willing spirit. / Then I will teach transgressors your ways, / and sinners will return to you." A constant willingness to repent and to turn back to God's mercy is a model of steadfast faith seen in martyrs ancient and current. They teach us that discipleship offers us a sure hope that death, suffering, and violence are not the last words, but instead a sign of the fading powers of this world, conquered through the service of the Son, who leads us to eternal life.

Meditate on the example of Jesus. How has following Jesus shaped your response to suffering? Has it been difficult at times to follow the path of Jesus? What has allowed you to continue to follow even in light of suffering or persecution?

A LITTLE THING

Palm Sunday of the Lord's Passion

Readings: John 12:12-16; Isa 50:4-7; Ps 22:8-9, 17-18, 19-20, 23-24;
Phil 2:6-11; Mark 14:1–15:47

"What she has done will be told in remembrance of her."
(Mark 14:9)

If the gospel accounts stopped just after Jesus' entry into Jerusalem on Palm Sunday, how would you imagine the next few days playing out? The Gospel of John quotes Zechariah 9:9-10 as Jesus enters the city: "Look, your king is coming, / sitting on a donkey's colt!" The people were taking "branches of palm trees" and going "out to meet him, shouting, / 'Hosanna! / Blessed is the one who comes in the name of the Lord— / the King of Israel!'" The scene could easily be imagined as a hero's entry in advance of his great triumph soon to follow.

When Jesus entered Jerusalem, his disciples must have felt the same weight of expectations, the portent of what Jesus' entry meant, not just for themselves, but for everyone. If Jesus was the promised Messiah, the events to come were not just concerned with the realities of one Passover in Jerusalem or the fate of the people of Judah but with the world and, yes, the world to come. What could one do but wait with sharp expectancy for the world-historical events to unfold?

And yet one unnamed woman does more than wait. Her actions interpret not only Jesus' entry as the expected king but the sort of king Jesus must be. After his entrance into Jerusalem, Jesus went to Bethany. In Bethany, "a woman came with an alabaster jar of very costly ointment of nard, and she broke open the jar and poured the ointment on his head." In this action, she simply supports the reception accorded Jesus as he entered Jerusalem as the king. The *mashiach* (Greek, *christos*) is the "anointed one," and her actions tell us that she not only understands that Jesus is the anointed one but that she has a need or responsibility to anoint him. But who is she to anoint a king?

The people gathered around Jesus, however, ask a different question: "'Why was the ointment wasted in this way? For this ointment could have been sold for more than three hundred denarii, and the money given to the poor.' And they scolded her." Their question is not without merit, for in scolding her they probably were attempting to voice Jesus' concern for the poor seen throughout his ministry. Jesus asks another question, "Let her alone; why do you trouble her?"

Somehow the concerned disciples have missed something. "She has performed a good service for me. For you always have the poor with you, and you can show kindness to them whenever you wish; but you will not always have me." Jesus' response is not an attempt to mark out the permanence of poverty as a social problem but to note that her "good service for me" has focused proper attention on him. Whether or not she knows the full implications of what she has done, she has directed those present to see Jesus as the Messiah, to grasp his christological identity.

Her identification of Jesus as the Christ by anointing went deeper, however, than even she knew, for she could not have known that she had also anointed Jesus' body "beforehand for its burial." Faithful women will later seek to care for Jesus' broken body after his death in order to anoint it with burial spices, but they would not find a body. The unnamed woman, though, already had anointed Jesus not only as a king but as the humble King who emptied himself out in death.

The humility of Jesus is reflected by the generosity of this woman, who pours out all that she has as a witness for him. Who is she to anoint a king? Given the universal significance of Jesus' passion week, her anointing might seem a little thing, but it is the most any of us can do: she recognizes Jesus, and gives all she has for him, not understanding completely that her actions helped to prepare the King, first for his death and then for his triumph, but knowing somehow he is the Messiah.

The significance of her actions is felt when Jesus says, "Truly I tell you, wherever the good news is proclaimed in the whole world, what she has done will be told in remembrance of her." We, too, are called to recognize Jesus the Messiah in faith, not simply as a conquering hero but as a servant willing to give himself up to death for us.

Place yourself in Bethany at Simon's house. What is your response to the woman's anointing of Jesus? How are we offering all we have for Jesus today? Are we offering our most precious gifts to the Messiah?

An Empty Tomb

Easter Sunday

Readings: Acts 10:34a, 37-43; Ps 118:1-2, 16-17, 22-23;
1 Cor 5:6b-8; John 20:1-9

"For as yet they did not understand the scripture." (John 20:9)

All the gospels recall that on the second morning after Jesus was laid in the tomb, Mary Magdalene and other women were the first to arrive at the tomb to care for Jesus' body, but his body was not in the tomb. It would be a strange account to concoct. Why? James Dunn says in *Jesus Remembered*, "As is well known, in Middle Eastern society of the time women were not regarded as reliable witnesses: a woman's testimony in court was heavily discounted. And any report that Mary had formerly been demon-possessed (Luke 8:2) would hardly add credibility to any story attributed to her in particular. Why then attribute such testimony to women—unless that was what was remembered as being the case?" ([Grand Rapids, MI: Eerdmans, 2003], 832–33).

The account of Mary Magdalene as the first witness of the empty tomb was born of a powerful, consistent oral tradition among the earliest disciples. This is not the oral tradition of rote memorization, the sort that memorizes parables, prayers, teachings, and laws, which was also part of first-century Judaism. This is autobiographical memory, in which stories of personal experience are passed on, often colored by the emotional interpretation of those who experienced the events, which shapes the details recalled in the passing on of the accounts. All of those present remember and recount that Mary was there first.

According to John's gospel, "Early on the first day of the week, while it was still dark, Mary Magdalene came to the tomb and saw that the stone had been removed from the tomb. So she ran and went to Simon Peter and the other disciple, the one whom Jesus loved, and said to them, 'They have taken the Lord out of the tomb, and we do not know where they have laid him.' Then Peter and the other disciple set out and went toward the tomb."

The absence of the body does not necessarily mean that Jesus was raised. There are more ordinary explanations that come to mind: the disciples went to the wrong tomb and the body was somewhere else; they lied about the missing body; or someone stole the body and hid it.

Yet if Jesus' body had been available, it makes sense that those who opposed the teaching of Jesus' resurrection would have found it, or produced it had they stolen it, to the derision and embarrassment of the disciples. If the body had indeed been taken by Jesus' disciples or they had gone to the wrong tomb, the reality of Jesus' body itself would have come to light and the location of his dead body would have put an end to the claims of resurrection. Indeed, his tomb might have become a pilgrimage site, a place of veneration of a great teacher and prophet killed by the Roman authorities.

In John's gospel, Mary Magdalene reports the empty tomb to Peter and the other disciple. The two of them run to the tomb. "Then the other disciple, who reached the tomb first, also went in, and he saw and believed; for as yet they did not understand the scripture, that he must rise from the dead." The juxtaposition here captures the initial confusion of the empty tomb. The other disciple, also known as the Beloved Disciple, "saw and believed," while Peter and Mary "did not understand the scripture, that he must rise from the dead."

The Beloved Disciple alone initially recognizes the spiritual meaning of the empty tomb, but his understanding will soon be the foundation of the whole church, spurred by later encounters with the risen Lord. The resurrection of Jesus became the central message of the new community of disciples.

The early Christians knew that "they put him to death by hanging him on a tree" and they knew where Jesus' dead body was laid. When Mary Magdalene and the other disciples encountered the empty tomb, it became the first piece of evidence that "God raised him on the third day and allowed him to appear, not to all the people but to us who were chosen by God as witnesses." Later, these witnesses would eat and drink "with him after he rose from the dead." Only one last task remained: to bear witness that the empty tomb, the end of Jesus' story, was just the beginning.

Run to Jesus' tomb with Mary Magdalene. What do you think when you find the tomb empty? Can you imagine that Jesus has been raised from the dead? Do you sense the initial joy and excitement of the first disciples?

one HearT anD SOUL

Second Sunday of Easter

Readings: Acts 4:32-35; Ps 118:2-4, 13-15, 22-24;
1 John 5:1-6; John 20:19-31

"Blessed are those who have not seen and yet have come to believe."
(John 20:29)

Many Catholics today are rightfully dismayed by divisive arguments among fellow Christians over matters as diverse as liturgy, the pope, politics, and morality. Only the strong of heart dare venture near comment sections on certain Catholic websites. Such disagreements, oftentimes petty, sometimes significant, stand in sharp contrast to the second summary in the Acts of the Apostles on the state of the early church.

According to Acts, "Now the whole group of those who believed were of one heart and soul, and no one claimed private ownership of any possessions, but everything they owned was held in common. . . . There was not a needy person among them, for as many as owned lands or houses sold them and brought the proceeds of what was sold. They laid it at the apostles' feet, and it was distributed to each as any had need." It is a beautiful image of the early church, strengthened by the story of Barnabas, which immediately follows these verses and describes him giving to the church the money gained from selling a plot of land.

It is an ideal picture, which is soon shattered by the story of Ananias and Sapphira, who also decide to sell a plot of land but hold back some of the money for a rainy-day fund. Their behavior indicates a fissure among the early disciples and undercuts the claim that "everything they owned was held in common."

Why does Luke include this story in Acts 5? It is a shocking story—both Ananias and Sapphira separately fall down dead immediately after their deceit is revealed—but it speaks to reality. Even in the heady days of the apostles, people were already seeking their own way and hedging their bets on the church.

The period of Easter brings into sharp contrast the stumbling ways of the believers, a feature found throughout the church's history, and the steadfast love of God, which the psalmist tells us "endures forever." As steadfast as God is, so we are fickle in the ways of God. And yet, as fickle and capricious as believers might be, there is persistence among the disciples of Jesus, who get up, brush the dirt from their clothes, and move forward eager again to follow God in "one heart and soul."

The apostle Thomas gives us another image of the wavering disciple, but in this case one who remains in the fold. Thomas did not witness the risen Lord and so hedged his bets on the reality of the resurrection even as the other apostles were telling him, "We have seen the Lord." Why would they lie to him in his grief? Still, he said, "Unless I see the mark of the nails in his hands, and put my finger in the mark of the nails and my hand in his side, I will not believe."

Thomas persisted in his unbelief, unconvinced by the other apostles, until a week later, when Jesus' disciples "were again in the house, and Thomas was with them. Although the doors were shut, Jesus came and stood among them and said, 'Peace be with you.' Then he said to Thomas, 'Put your finger here and see my hands. Reach out your hand and put it in my side. Do not doubt but believe.'" Only then did Thomas answer, "My Lord and my God!"

How did the other disciples treat Thomas during that week? It seems that they did not cast him out for doubting, marginalize him, or call him a "cafeteria apostle" but allowed him to remain with them. For his part, Thomas stayed with them, even in the midst of his doubt.

We all need and rely on the steadfastness of God at all times to support us when we are uncertain, but the support of other believers is essential, not "even" when we disagree, but especially when we disagree. Thomas did not believe initially and only believed when he saw Jesus in the risen flesh. "Jesus said to him, 'Have you believed because you have seen me? Blessed are those who have not seen and yet have come to believe.'" Important in all of this, though, and often overlooked, is that in the midst of Thomas's profound disagreement with the other disciples regarding Jesus' resurrection, he remained within the fold of the brothers and sisters.

Consider the doubt of Thomas and remember he remained with his fellow disciples. How can you help to build up a church of one heart and one soul? How do you treat those with whom you disagree? Can you do something to bring others back to the fold?

our witnesses

Third Sunday of Easter

Readings: Acts 3:13-15, 17-19; Ps 4:2, 4, 7-8, 9;
1 John 2:1-5a; Luke 24:35-48

"You are witnesses of these things." (Luke 24:48)

To what do the apostles and the other disciples witness when they are called to be witnesses to Jesus Christ? On the one hand, they bear witness to his death: "But you rejected the Holy and Righteous One and asked to have a murderer given to you, and you killed the Author of life." Yet, even here, the witness to the crucifixion is tied intimately to the resurrection, for the verse continues, "whom God raised from the dead. To this we are witnesses." The importance of being witnesses to the resurrection is stressed also at the end of the Gospel of Luke.

After the events on the road to Emmaus, the disciples were gathered and witnessed Jesus walking, talking, and eating among them. While initially "they were startled and terrified, and thought that they were seeing a ghost," they were soon convinced that Jesus was alive: "'Why are you frightened, and why do doubts arise in your hearts? Look at my hands and my feet; see that it is I myself. Touch me and see; for a ghost does not have flesh and bones as you see that I have.' And when he had said this, he showed them his hands and his feet."

Luke tells us that "in their joy they were disbelieving and still wondering." What a terrific description! It evokes a sense of someone holding a newborn for the first time, a team winning an improbable victory, or finding out you got the job. Is this real, or is it just a dream?

Then Jesus did the most human of things to ground them: "Have you anything here to eat?" The Greek of the NRSV seems too formal. I would opt for "What do you guys have to eat here?" They gave Jesus "a piece of broiled fish, and he took it and ate in their presence." Things just got real.

Jesus once again explained his death, its necessity and its connection to the resurrection. "Thus it is written, that the Messiah is to suffer and to rise from the dead on the third day, and that repentance and forgiveness of sins is to be proclaimed in his name to all nations, beginning from Jerusalem. You are witnesses of these things." That makes sense. They actually were witnesses to these things, they actually saw him die, ate with him, talked to him, felt the giddy excitement of his presence.

But to what are we witnesses today? None of us saw him die on the cross, or watched him eat that piece of broiled fish, feeling faint with joy and amazement as we saw him alive in our midst. We are witness to two things: the authenticity and trustworthiness of the witnesses, and the authenticity and trustworthiness of our lives.

In our lives, we have choices each day. And as John says, "My little children, I am writing these things to you so that you may not sin." Not to sin would be the best path, but our weaknesses lead us astray. Still, because of Jesus' death and resurrection, "if anyone does sin, we have an advocate with the Father, Jesus Christ the righteous; and he is the atoning sacrifice for our sins, and not for ours only but also for the sins of the whole world." Whenever we struggle with sin—so often the same old boring sins, so dull and stupid—"we may be sure that we know him, if we obey his commandments." We can turn back to the commandments and we must turn back to the commandments and live them out in our lives. If we do not, John tells us, each of us becomes "a liar," but we have the ability to show the world the reality of the risen Lord through our love, our obedience, our tenderness, our mercy, our gentleness, our desire to live out and witness to Christ's victory through our daily choices.

And we bear witness to the one who was raised from the dead when we believe the words the apostles passed on to us. We believe in their trustworthiness about Jesus because we live out their love for Jesus. When we live as Jesus asked us to, passed on to us by the tradition, "by this we may be sure that we are in him." How we live makes us witnesses to Jesus Christ. It is our task today to bear witness.

In your imagination, gather with the disciples after the experience on the road to Emmaus. Do you ever experience the wonder of the first disciples? How do you bear witness to the risen Lord? In what way can your witness grow?

THe SHePHerD'S LoVe

Fourth Sunday of Easter

Readings: Acts 4:8-12; Ps 118:1, 8-9, 21-23, 26, 28, 29;
1 John 3:1-2; John 10:11-18

"The hired hand runs away because a hired hand
does not care for the sheep." (John 10:13)

In 2 Esdras, a Jewish apocalyptic text of the first century AD, Ezra is asked by "Phaltiel, a chief of the people," whether he knows "that Israel has been entrusted to you in the land of their exile? Rise therefore and eat some bread, and do not forsake us, like a shepherd who leaves the flock in the power of savage wolves" (5:16-18). The image is similar to that found in the Gospel of John, in which Jesus says, "I am the good shepherd. The good shepherd lays down his life for the sheep. The hired hand, who is not the shepherd and does not own the sheep, sees the wolf coming and leaves the sheep and runs away—and the wolf snatches them and scatters them. The hired hand runs away because a hired hand does not care for the sheep."

In *Let the Little Children Come to Me*, Cornelia Horn and I wrote that "the account of the Good Shepherd in John 10 offers a theological image of Jesus' love for his people, but its relevance as a metaphor for Jesus' love derives from the ability to connect the image to everyday instances taken from life. Jesus is not a 'hired worker' (*misthōtos*), but rather someone who cares for the sheep, who will lay down his life for the sheep (John 10:11-15). What, in contrast, will the hired worker do when the wolf comes? He (or she) will run" ([Washington, DC: CUA Press, 2009], 178).

But the hired hands also function quite clearly on a metaphoric level, which Jesus draws out explicitly. If he is the Good Shepherd, who are the hired hands? They are synonymous, as in 2 Esdras, with Jewish religious authorities who do not care for the sheep as a good shepherd. Based in an actual agricultural image, which ordinary people knew intimately, the condemnation of these hired hands is grounded in day-to-day life.

43

Jesus cares for the people, the sheep, because they are his sheep and Jesus will protect them. This much is clear, yet the extension of the image seems bizarre, when Jesus says, "And I lay down my life for the sheep." Are the sheep worth it? Are the sheep worth dying for? And if the shepherd dies for his sheep, who will protect them? This image shines a light on the absurdity of Jesus' sacrifice for humanity. For this sacrifice makes sense only if through it the flock will be better protected.

And this is the case as Jesus speaks of his death, which will lead to bringing in "other sheep that do not belong to this fold . . . So there will be one flock, one shepherd." Jesus does speak of laying down his life, but it is "in order to take it up again. No one takes it from me, but I lay it down of my own accord. I have power to lay it down, and I have power to take it up again. I have received this command from my Father." At first blush, dying for the sheep seems to run counter to the goal of caring for the sheep, but it is the reason for the flock's flourishing today all over the world.

The results are seen when the "rulers of the people and elders" question Peter as to how a lame man was healed; he answers that his restoration to wholeness was "by the name of Jesus Christ of Nazareth, whom you crucified, whom God raised from the dead. This Jesus is / 'the stone that was rejected by you, the builders; / it has become the cornerstone.' / There is salvation in no one else, for there is no other name under heaven given among mortals by which we must be saved."

Not only has the Good Shepherd saved the sheep through giving his life up for them, but he has emboldened the flock itself, no longer to be sheep, but "that we should be called children of God; and that is what we are . . . Beloved, we are God's children now; what we will be has not yet been revealed. What we do know is this: when he is revealed, we will be like him, for we will see him as he is." We have been saved to become children, but our final goal, which we cannot yet fully imagine, is to become like the Good Shepherd.

Reflect on these images: What does it mean for you to be a part of Jesus' flock? What does it mean to be a child of God? What image speaks to you most fully?

DISCIPLES I Fear

Fifth Sunday of Easter

Readings: Acts 9:26-31; Ps 22:26-27, 28, 30, 31-32;
1 John 3:18-24; John 15:1-8

*"They were all afraid of him, for they did not
believe that he was a disciple."* (Acts 9:26)

We might not say it outright, although unfortunately many of us do, but we are often not convinced that so-and-so is a true Christian. We might know the person well, by public reputation or just by name, or we might not know the name of the person at all who bothers us, or worse, with their words and behavior. From a friend's Facebook post came this comment about a Catholic politician: "You can't be Catholic if . . . And this is one of those ifs." Thank goodness we can now determine the state of a person's soul on Facebook.

Yet this social media response is similar to the one Paul evoked when the Christians "were all afraid of him, for they did not believe that he was a disciple." Now it is true that when Paul was creating fear in the hearts of the Christians of Damascus and Antioch, they had good reasons to fear him. Paul was a persecutor of the church who had officially aided in the killing of Stephen. How could they be sure Paul was not intending to trap them?

There are, frankly, reasons to mistrust certain people because of their behavior and beliefs; and even forgiveness, the heart of the church's mission, does not mean people should be restored to positions of authority or trust in the church or society if they have breached that trust grievously. But we do need to ask ourselves how we are judging people within the church, our brothers and sisters, or those outside the church, called to be one family with us, and whether it is the product of true discernment or simply gossip, fear, and bias.

In many and various ways, we question the reality or sincerity of our brothers' and sisters' beliefs and actions, sometimes because of actual bad behavior, sometimes because of incomplete information, and sometimes just because we do not like that person.

Our judgment, in fact, often expresses implicit doubt about God's grace and its ability to transform and convert even the most hardened soul. Or we are judging on partial information or just a human propensity to prefer certain people over other people. Some people just bug us for no real reason.

Barnabas defended Paul, reporting that Paul had an encounter with the risen Lord, "who had spoken to him," and that in Damascus "he had spoken boldly in the name of Jesus." Paul had been transformed by God's grace from a man willing to kill to impose his view of God, to one willing to be killed in order to evangelize.

Are we allowing that God can work in peoples' hearts and souls? Paul was worthy of trust because he acted out the Gospel "not in word or speech, but in truth and action." We are asked by God to "obey his commandments and do what pleases him. And this is his commandment, that we should believe in the name of his Son Jesus Christ and love one another, just as he has commanded us." When we judge our brothers and sisters as not measuring up to the commandments, are we loving them? Do we judge ourselves with the same sharp eye for mistakes that we have for those of others? Are we praying for the conversion of others and ourselves?

There is indeed judgment. There can be no truth or justice without it, but we often set ourselves as the true arbiters of judgment, even if it is in the quietness of our hearts where we whisper condemnation of the "others," however we may categorize and group them. But this is not our personal task. Jesus is "the true vine" and God "is the vinegrower." It is God who "removes every branch . . . that bears no fruit. Every branch that bears fruit he prunes to make it bear more fruit." We have no need to condemn, for we do not know how God is pruning others or ourselves, preparing us to flourish in growth and fruitfulness.

God looks at us, whoever we are, at whatever point we are in our lives, however far we have strayed, and asks that we "bear much fruit and become my disciples." Do not fear the other disciples; just attempt to become one more firmly rooted in the soil that nourishes us all, entwined with the vine and pruned by the loving hands of the vinegrower.

Think of a disciple whom you fear or reject. How can you learn to love this brother or sister? What have you done to understand this person? How have you reached out to him or her?

Same as it ever was?

Sixth Sunday of Easter

Readings: Acts 10:25-26, 34-35, 44-48; Ps 98:1, 2-3, 3-4;
1 John 4:7-10; John 15:9-17

"I truly understand that God shows no partiality." (Acts 10:34)

In the Talking Heads song "Once in a Lifetime," the refrain repeats over and over: "Same as it ever was, same as it ever was . . ." Whether the refrain is meant to reflect the constancy of sameness or the inevitability of change is an open question. There is in life a tension between the predictability of change and growth and the permanence and stability of reality. The Easter experience of the apostles reveals to us a number of ancient examples that bear witness to the tension between permanence and change.

We know that God is the same as God ever was, unchanging and eternal, revealed to Moses as "I AM WHO I AM" (Exod 3:14). At the heart of God's unchanging being are unity and love. Yet the way in which God's unity and love were revealed to the apostles and the disciples of the earliest church shattered expectations about the nature of God. By the sending of God's own Son, Jesus Christ, to save us through the conquest of death and sin, and then in the giving of the Holy Spirit to comfort and guide the church, something had changed about how we knew and experienced God's being and love.

It is not that the love of God was new to the Jews. As the First Letter of John expresses it, "let us love one another, because love is from God; everyone who loves is born of God and knows God." God's love had been made manifest throughout Israel's history. Yet "God's love was revealed among us in this way: God sent his only Son into the world so that we might live through him." In the manifestation of God's son, something new had happened.

The newness is found in the growth of the post-Easter church as it tried to make sense of what Jesus had wrought not just for his small group of disciples but for all humanity. There was not a clear-cut path for the church, a blueprint or manual that laid out a five-year plan for church growth. What the apostles had was the gift of the Holy Spirit to help them make sense of their mission and to discover what the church was to be.

There is an inherent wildness in the Holy Spirit, a sort of untamable or unmanageable nature, and the work of the Holy Spirit can challenge old ways of thinking and acting. It certainly challenged the early church, as we see in the extended encounter between Peter and Cornelius in the Acts of the Apostles.

By means of visions, prayer, and the experience of the Holy Spirit, Peter is brought to a new realization: God has given the Holy Spirit even to the Gentiles. If this does not seem shocking, it is because we have lost the sense of wonder shared by Peter and the apostles that even the Gentiles can be saved. But Peter's shock registers throughout Acts 10.

The newness of Gentile inclusion resonates throughout Peter's proclamation: "I truly understand that God shows no partiality, but in every nation anyone who fears him and does what is right is acceptable to him." This is new, something radically new, head-spinning even, for a new path is being cleared for the universal mission of the church. Peter does not wait to consult with the other apostles, but acts on the experience of the Holy Spirit in their midst. "Can anyone withhold the water for baptizing these people who have received the Holy Spirit just as we have?" Peter definitely could not. He did it. He baptized them.

One cannot deny the shocking change that came upon the disciples of Jesus through the Holy Spirit and the newness of Gentile inclusion, although Peter's quick decision would need to be ratified by the church in the council at Jerusalem. But this newness also found its resting place in the state of permanence, that is, the unchanging love of God. For what the church was called to do was to bring to the whole world the call to keep God's commandment, something old, made new in the revelation of the Son and the Holy Spirit. "This is my commandment, that you love one another as I have loved you"—this love of God and neighbor, the same as it ever was and made completely new.

Imagine yourself with Peter and Cornelius. How would you have reacted to God doing something new? Would you have welcomed this change or balked at it? How is the Holy Spirit doing a new thing today in your life or in the world?

WHaT TIMe IT IS

The Ascension of the Lord

Readings: Acts 1:1-11; Ps 47:2-3, 6-7, 8-9;
Eph 1:17-23; Mark 16:15-20

"Lord, is this the time when you will restore the kingdom to Israel?"
(Acts 1:6)

Still reeling from the trauma of the crucifixion and then the shattering of all earthly expectations by Jesus' resurrection from the dead, the apostles, trying to make sense of the common Jewish beliefs regarding the Messiah and the apocalyptic establishment of God's kingdom, pose a simple question to Jesus prior to his ascension: "Lord, is this the time when you will restore the kingdom to Israel?"

Implicit in this question is a desire to understand what comes next. If God's ways had left them confounded and confused, yet still elated, could they now grasp the order of the next events? Would the plan follow what they understood the pattern of the coming kingdom of God to be? Not exactly. For Jesus tells them, "It is not for you to know the times or periods that the Father has set by his own authority." All they needed to know was that they were to be witnesses to the life and resurrection of Jesus and were to bring their witness to the truth of Christ to the world, beginning from Jerusalem, Judea, and Samaria to the ends of the earth. Whatever came next would have to be discovered in the course of faithfully carrying out their mission.

It was not that Jesus was not who they thought he was—though they would discover he was more than they could have imagined, namely, God incarnate. It was that "the earliest Christian community had to *discover* that God's saving act temporally differentiated the enthronement of the Son of man from his judgment of the world; it had to *discover* that the Gentiles' share in this same saving act demanded the launching of a world mission" (Ben F. Meyer, *The Aims of Jesus* [Eugene, OR: Wipf and Stock, 2002], 109). It was in the experience of living their lives as faithful disciples of Jesus that they would come to understand how the events of Jesus' life informed their task as church.

Jesus' ascension might be the most misunderstood and overlooked of the events remembered during the Easter season, from the resurrection to Pentecost. But the story of the ascension, which is cast in the language of ancient cosmology, with Jesus "going up" to heaven, is about the enthronement of Christ as Lord. The Gospel of Mark will describe Jesus as "taken up into heaven and sat down at the right hand of God."

The apostles' previous hope that Jesus should now restore the kingdom to Israel in a physical sense would now be understood as Jesus' enthronement as the king who rules with authority over all temporal and spiritual powers. Not only was Jesus King of Israel but he was, indeed, King of the world.

The Letter to the Ephesians relates that God's power was at work in Christ through the resurrection and when God "seated him at his right hand in the heavenly places, far above all rule and authority and power and dominion, and above every name that is named, not only in this age but also in the age to come." It is because Christ already rules that he is able to guide the church in wisdom and enlightenment, but even more to focus our hope on the kingdom still to come in its full glory. This power is at work even now in the Body of Christ here on earth, the church, allowing it to continue Jesus' mission of proclamation for the salvation of the world.

The apostles asked, "Lord, is this the time when you will restore the kingdom to Israel?" Jesus' rejoinder to the apostles, to focus on their own task as church, is not a denial of his kingship but the means by which Jesus' kingship would be made known universally.

Yes, the kingdom came in a way they never expected. As we reflect that "this Jesus, who has been taken up from you into heaven, will come in the same way as you saw him go into heaven," we also wonder, when will that be?

Like Peter and the other apostles, we have our tasks as witnesses, while we await in hope the fullness of the kingdom, knowing that the one who promised it will do it. He will fulfill our hopes beyond our wildest expectations. We do not know when or how this will be, but the one who promised it already reigns, and he will do it in ways we have never imagined.

Ponder Jesus' ascension. How does Jesus' ascension help you understand the church's mission? How does the ascension give you hope? Does the ascension change your understanding of Jesus' kingship?

THE FELLOWSHIP OF THE HOLY SPIRIT

Seventh Sunday of Easter

Readings: Acts 1:15-17, 20a, 20c-26; Ps 103:1-2, 11-12, 19-20;
1 John 4:11-16; John 17:11b-19

> *"Beloved, since God loved us so much,*
> *we also ought to love one another."* (1 John 4:11)

When things are going well, in the flush of excitement or accomplishment, it can be easy to be everyone's friend. Character is revealed when everything has gone south, when friends are nowhere to be found, divisions are revealed, and struggles abound. It is hard to compare Pentecost, or the aftermath of Pentecost, as simply a time of excitement or joy, though it does encompass these human emotions. Pentecost surpassed human emotion as it was indeed an event that transcended ordinary human hopes and joys. The coming of the Holy Spirit established the church not in the vicissitudes of warm feelings, but in the stability of divinity.

This stability leads us to a certitude in belief. When the Holy Spirit came to the apostle Paul personally it so transformed him as to turn his life around forever. Yet, being convinced of the truth of God's work in the church and in each other does not relieve us of our humanity. It is also the case that life, even in the continuing exhilaration of Pentecost, has a way of impinging on the warmth and oneness that emanates from peak experiences. Paul might have done a theological 180 degree turn, but he remained as feisty as ever in his personal relationships. Paul's theological battles, described in Acts of the Apostles and in his own letters, mark him as human.

While the church drew on the guidance of the Holy Spirit in the choice of Joseph Barsabbas, also known as Justus, to become an apostle in the heady days after Pentecost, the choice was only necessary, as we all know, because of the betrayal of Judas Iscariot at the heart of Jesus' own inner circle. Whenever we reflect on dark divisions in the church in our own day, we must remember that even one of Jesus' closest friends turned on him. The temptation to turn to our own ways is not a product of modernity, or modern political divisions, but inherent in the human condition, ravaged by sin and selfishness. It is a constant lesson, which we must relearn daily, that the oneness Christ established for the church is an exercise that must be enacted in each heart and soul.

The lesson is learned from the reality, as John says, that "since God loved us so much, we also ought to love one another. No one has ever seen God; if we love one another, God lives in us, and his love is perfected in us." In the constant living out of love, we make manifest God in us and God with us. When John says that "no one has ever seen God" in this context, the point seems to be that it is only by showing love that we can show God to our brothers and sisters and the world around us. It might supply an answer to a baffling question as to why Paul, in Galatians 5:14, writes, "For the whole law is summed up in a single commandment, 'You shall love your neighbor as yourself,' " while omitting the command to love God as well, as Jesus taught us from Deuteronomy 6:4. My sense, though, is that Paul knows that if one cannot demonstrate love of neighbor, talk of loving God is only so much talk. In the loving of the neighbor, God's love and the reality of God is made evident.

All of this, of course, is an attempt to answer how we create unity in the church when the times of the Holy Spirit moving among us seem distant and unreal. But it is not up to us to "create" unity, but only grasp the Holy Spirit, who is always with us, and the unity of God. We wander as individuals away from God's will for us, away from God's working in us, when we pay attention more to our own desires than those of God's. Naturally, as human beings, troubles occur and anger flares up. Jesus prays in the farewell discourse in the Gospel of John, though, that God protect his flock "so that they may be one, as we are one." We do, of course, have to align ourselves with God's will in order to live out this oneness with God, but this is where church unity emerges.

The temptations to turn from living out unity does not come from this Catholic group or another, but from within each of us, attempting to seek our own path like Judas. What turns us from the way of God are not disputes and arguments that come from the process of discernment, and are natural to the life of the church, but from the evil one, just as Judas was hoodwinked. It is in the dehumanizing of those with whom we disagree that we turn from the Holy Spirit. Jesus prayed to the Father, "I am not asking you to take them out of the world, but I ask you to protect them from the evil one. They do not belong to the world, just as I do not belong to the world. Sanctify them in the truth; your word is truth." Only the truth of God, found in turning from our own ways to the path of love of God and love of neighbor, brings us to unity, because it brings us into the heart of God.

Contemplate how you might work for unity in the church. Are you moving outside of your comfort zone to reach out to those with whom you disagree? Are you discerning the spirits in your own choices and decisions? How might you more fully act in love today?

THe SPIrIT OF TruTH COmes

Pentecost Sunday

Readings: Acts 2:1-11; Ps 104:1, 24, 29-30, 31, 34;
1 Cor 12:3b-7, 12-13; John 15:26-27; 16:12-15

"When the Spirit of truth comes, he will guide you into all the truth."
(John 16:13)

The Greek word *pneuma* can be translated "wind, breath, or spirit." So when the sound at the door is "like the rush of a violent wind," you should answer, and you had better be prepared to have your world turned upside down. Or right-side up. Because according to the Acts of the Apostles, that would be the Holy Spirit announcing its coming; and as Jesus promised in the Gospel of John, the Holy Spirit is the "Spirit of truth," who "will guide you into all the truth." The truth is not necessarily staid, polite, reticent, and reserved. It tends to rock the world and shake up expectations.

On Pentecost, the disciples of Jesus were all together in a house when the Holy Spirit blew in with a charismatic plan of action that I suspect was not previously on their minds. The ensuing commotion was so loud and raucous that a crowd gathered outside, and some of the crowd suggested that perhaps the disciples of Jesus had been drinking that morning (Acts 2:13). It was not alcohol that fueled them, though, but the Holy Spirit showing them in deed some of the truths about what it meant to be the church.

First, the disciples "were filled with the Holy Spirit and began to speak in other languages, as the Spirit gave them ability." These languages, heard by others in their own native tongues, were a clear sign that the church was not simply a phenomenon meant for a small corner of the world, but for all people. The church's mission was to be universal.

Second, the Holy Spirit drew an "amazed and astonished" crowd. Some of them sneered at the disciples, but the majority were attracted to this strange witness of God. The crowds were open to the truth because they had witnessed the power of the Holy Spirit in their midst and the joy of the disciples.

But while the truth always shakes up the world, the Holy Spirit does not always come like a violent wind. The charism of tongues and the presence of large crowds clamoring to find out what is going on are not essential to the work of the Holy Spirit; the Holy Spirit can come quietly, gently, like a light breeze.

Some gifts are so subtle that they go unnoticed by the crowd. The Holy Spirit has so infused the lives of some Christians that their kind words, loving service, moral support, and listening ear change lives in the quietest of ways. Apart from the din of crowds, their gifts emanate gently to all who encounter them. A kind word can be "the utterance of knowledge," a shoulder to cry on "the utterance of wisdom," and "all these are activated by one and the same Spirit, who allots to each one individually just as the Spirit chooses."

The apostle Paul speaks of the variety of gifts given to the Body of Christ through its individual members. While some of these charisms might seem like "greater" spiritual gifts, like the working of miracles, prophecy, discernment of spirits, tongues, and the interpretation of tongues, Paul stresses that though there are varieties of gifts, services, and activities, there is "the same Spirit," "the same Lord," "the same God who activates all of them in everyone," and it is God's love that is the foundation for all of them.

The Holy Spirit might shake you up, like a rush of the wind knocking at the door, or calm you down, by the comforting movement of grace; we experience today the same Spirit Jesus gave to the apostles and that brought them together in unity at Pentecost. That same Spirit of truth is here now, manifested in the lives of your brothers and sisters and in you.

Each of us has gifts, and we never know when they are needed or how they affect the common good of the church and the world. We need to be ready to experience the Holy Spirit at all times, both by receiving the gifts of others and by offering our gifts to others. Listen, for the Holy Spirit always comes, and you should always be ready to respond to the call. Even if it does turn your world upside down. Or right-side up.

Imagine yourself at the first Pentecost. What do you imagine your response would be to the coming of the Holy Spirit? How would you translate that excitement and joy into your daily life? How is this same Spirit guiding you, your parish, and the universal church today?

ADOPTED INTO THE FAMILY OF GOD

The Solemnity of the Most Holy Trinity

Readings: Deut 4:32-34, 39-40; Ps 33:4-5, 6, 9, 18-19, 20, 22; Rom 8:14-17; Matt 28:16-20

"For all who are led by the Spirit of God are children of God."
(Rom 8:14)

God chose the Israelites to be his people, his nation, his children. And so they are his children, a family established through the covenant God ratified with Abraham. At the heart of the covenant was the understanding that Israel "would acknowledge that the Lord is God" and that they would "keep his statutes and his commandments, which I am commanding you today for your own well-being and that of your descendants after you."

The descendants of Abraham who had heard God's call of election and embraced it were God's chosen people. Yet the world was full of other people, also created by God, also beloved by God. From the beginning of the covenantal relationship, Abraham was told "no one but your very own issue shall be your heir" (Gen 15:4). But there was an additional promise: "In you all the families of the earth shall be blessed" (Gen 12:3). How would God be revealed to the other families of the earth? How would the other families of the earth enter the covenant and become heirs to the promises of God?

The language of families here is significant, for it is through the revelation of God as Trinity, the divine family, that all other families of the earth would be invited into the covenant family. For the reality of the Trinity did not emerge for the earliest Christians in the context of complex philosophical discussions but in the experience of God as Father, Son, and Holy Spirit. As Pope Benedict XVI stated in 2006, "the intimacy of God himself, discovering that he is not infinite solitude but communion of light and love, life given and received in an eternal dialogue between the Father and the Son in the Holy Spirit—Lover, Loved and Love," revealed the relational nature of God through the guidance of the Holy Spirit and by the incarnation of Jesus Christ (Angelus, St. Peter's Square, June 11, 2006).

And it was by means of the revelation of God as Father, Son, and Holy Spirit that the early Christians came to know themselves as children of God, adopted into the family and covenant of God. The Spirit, Paul tells us, empowers us to understand that we too are children of God, for through the Spirit we are able to cry "Abba! Father!" This Spirit-infused call to God as Abba is an explicit recognition of our lineage: we belong in this family, for "it is that very Spirit bearing witness with our spirit that we are children of God."

But the pathway to entering the family as heirs—children destined to share in the gifts and promises of the Father in the kingdom of God—was blazed for us by the obedience of the Son. As Paul says in Galatians 3:29, "If you belong to Christ, then you are Abraham's offspring, heirs according to the promise." Christ, through his suffering and death for us, has made us "joint heirs with Christ," worthy of adoption into God's family. The Greek for "heir," *klēronomos*, is combined with the Greek for "with" to make *synklēronomos*, "joint heirs." We belong to the family of God because we belong to the Son, who has made us "joint heirs." Through the true "heir" we are simply joined with our covenantal and divine family.

We are welcomed into God's family as joint heirs because of the love of the Trinity for us. The Trinity models the nature of the family by allowing us to experience the source of all love. It is because of the trinitarian model of love for us and our experience of that love that Jesus instructs us to go out and make the family bigger. We belong in the family of God, but so do those who have not yet come home.

When Jesus instructs the apostles to go out, "baptizing them in the name of the Father and of the Son and of the Holy Spirit, and teaching them to obey everything that I have commanded you," it is only an expansion of the covenant call to Abraham and the people of Israel to "acknowledge that the LORD is God" and to "keep his statutes and his commandments." True, we have learned something new about the nature of God and the extent of God's family, but the call is the same: come home and be loved.

Reflect on the nature of the Trinity. Does the revelation of the Trinity help you understand the nature of your family and the family of God? What does it mean to you to be an "heir" in God's family? Do you understand the church as family?

Bread of Heaven

**The Solemnity of the Most Holy Body
and Blood of Christ**

Readings: Exod 24:3-8; Ps 116:12-13, 15-16, 17-18;
Heb 9:11-15; Mark 14:12-16, 22-26

"I am the living bread that came down from heaven." (John 6:51)

Sometimes I find myself in a lineup with a bunch of strangers, shuffling down the aisle in church, and I forget that I am standing with my family on the pathway to heaven about to partake of the Body and Blood of Christ offered once for all time for the salvation of the world. Perhaps you have walked down that aisle with me?

The sacrificial nature of the Eucharist is clear from Jesus' words and actions at the Last Supper, but hearing the words of institution over and over can become a part of a rote behavior that obscures their life-giving meaning. In the words of Mark's gospel, "While they were eating, he took a loaf of bread, and after blessing it he broke it, gave it to them, and said, 'Take; this is my body.' Then he took a cup, and after giving thanks he gave it to them, and all of them drank from it. He said to them, 'This is my blood of the covenant, which is poured out for many.'"

The primary sacrificial context for the Last Supper comes from the Passover feast in which the meal is situated, but the offering of Jesus' Body and Blood on behalf of the "many"—that is, for all people—takes on and reinterprets much more of the sacrificial imagery of the Old Testament. The bread that he broke is a sign of his body, which he will offer in death, the true bread of the presence. The "blood of the covenant" shares in the imagery of the ceremony in Exodus in which Moses sprinkled blood on the people of Israel as a sign of their obedience to the covenant. The phrase "poured out for many" draws us inexorably to the Suffering Servant of Isaiah 53:12, who pours himself out as an expiation for the sins of the people.

These sacrificial realities are not alien to the Last Supper. They are an inherent part of Jesus' actions, which he interprets for his apostles prior to the crucifixion. But for these understandings to come to the fore, the first Christians had to meditate and reflect on what Jesus had done and what this meant for the continuing life of the church.

The author of the Letter to the Hebrews makes it his mission to explicate and explain what took place on Calvary in light of the Jewish sacrificial system. First, Hebrews explains that Jesus is not only the sacrifice for the sins of the world but also the perfect high priest. Second, the perfect high priest "entered once for all into the Holy Place, not with the blood of goats and calves, but with his own blood, thus obtaining eternal redemption." Third, through the offering of himself as the perfect sacrifice, Jesus "is the mediator of a new covenant, so that those who are called may receive the promised eternal inheritance."

Joachim Jeremias wrote in *The Eucharistic Words of Jesus*, "If, immediately following his words on the bread and immediately following his words on the wine, Jesus gives the same bread and the same wine to his disciples, this act signifies his giving them a share, by their eating and drinking, in the atoning power of his death" ([New York: Scribner, 1966], 233). And that atoning power has as its goal eternal life with Jesus. But it was not just those who sat at the table with Jesus and ate bread and drank wine with him who are able to share in the atoning power of Jesus' sacrifice; Jesus opened the way for all to share in the eternal inheritance.

The Eucharist fulfills the sacrificial system and gives us the ability to share in the power of Christ's atoning death here and now, but it also prepares us for our eternal inheritance. With the rest of God's family, we will share in the messianic banquet. Jesus tells us "many will come from east and west and will eat with Abraham and Isaac and Jacob in the kingdom of heaven" (Matt 8:11). Only the true bread of heaven, the perfect High Priest, could offer himself once for all and so pave the way for our entry into the temple made not with hands. So walk with joy toward the temple prepared for us for eternity, as you are about to share a foretaste of the unending banquet.

Meditate on the Last Supper. How does your participation in the Body and Blood of Christ shape your Christian life? Are you focused on the reality of Christ's sacrifice? Are you always aware that you are participating in the heavenly banquet even now?

women together

The Assumption of the Blessed Virgin Mary

Readings: Rev 11:19a; 12:1-6a, 10ab; Ps 45:10, 11, 12, 16;
1 Cor 15:20-27; Luke 1:39-56

*"And Mary remained with her about three months
and then returned to her home."* (Luke 1:56)

The assumption of Mary into heaven, an event that is not described in the biblical tradition, has nevertheless been a part of the church's tradition, east and west, since the early centuries. It emerged out of reflection among the faithful on the profound role Mary had in the salvation of all humanity, especially in her openness and faithfulness to God. Her openness and faithfulness to God were most profoundly witnessed in her bearing and giving birth to the Son of God, her son Jesus. It was understood that her role in the divine plan warranted her being taken bodily to heaven, to be in the home of God, the one to whom she gave a home in God's earthly sojourn.

Some have seen support for the church's teaching regarding Mary in the image of the "woman clothed with the sun" in Revelation. In this mythic imagery, a woman appears "with the moon under her feet, and on her head a crown of twelve stars. She was pregnant and was crying out in birth pangs, in the agony of giving birth" (12:1-2). Others have rejected this image because the woman "was crying out in birth pangs," thinking, according to other ancient noncanonical Marian texts, that Mary had no birth pangs when she gave birth to Jesus. It is best, however, not to read the images of Revelation, or these noncanonical texts, such as the Protoevangelium of James, too literally.

The woman certainly could stand for Mary, since the woman "gave birth to a son, a male child, who is to rule all the nations with a rod of iron" (12:5). But like so many images in Revelation, the symbol is polyvalent, having more than one referent. Remember, the woman had "on her head a crown of twelve stars," which could signify the twelve tribes of Israel or the twelve apostles, so referencing the church. Later, the woman "fled into the wilderness, where she has a place prepared by God, so that there she can be nourished for one thousand two hundred sixty days" (12:6). This most certainly is a reference to the church, as the "one thousand two hundred sixty days" refers to a symbolic number in Daniel regarding a period of three and a half years before the time of the end.

The point is that Mary is in heaven with her Lord and she is not simply the stuff of legendary, mythic, or symbolic numbers. She was a woman, an actual flesh and blood woman, chosen above all people, male or female, to play the most significant human role in the divine salvific plan. We should never lose track of her humanity and distance Mary from ourselves or specifically the women of the world. There is this temptation to dehumanize her, but this pays no justice to her faithfulness or to Mary as a model woman, someone women and men can follow as exemplary in trust and joy.

As a model for women, we should note that when Mary heard the word from the angel, she went to confide in another woman, not in the men of her family. She traveled "with haste" to the Judean hill country to see her relative Elizabeth. It was Elizabeth to whom Mary entrusted her momentous news and Elizabeth, far from questioning Mary, was open to Mary and her greeting. The Holy Spirit filled Elizabeth and she cried out, "Blessed are you among women, and blessed is the fruit of your womb. And why has this happened to me, that the mother of my Lord comes to me?"

Elizabeth was there for Mary, open to her joy and faithfulness, open to being with her and listening to her story. It was in response to Elizabeth's belief, recall, that Mary recited the *Magnificat*. In this song of praise, Mary speaks of her joy at being chosen, of being blessed in spite of what she calls "the lowliness of his servant." More significantly, Mary places her own role in the context of God's promises and faithfulness to the people of Israel and the lowly and forgotten of the world. So often the lowly and the forgotten in the world are comprised of women, like Mary and Elizabeth, whose roles are denigrated and whose bodies bear the brunt of abuse and pain.

Mary did not just stop by to talk to Elizabeth; she needed to stay with Elizabeth and so "Mary remained with her about three months and then returned to her home." They were women together because though Mary had been called and chosen for a role unique among women, had been set apart to return bodily to God's kingdom, she needed another woman, a friend and relative, to talk to, to be with, to share her story.

Contemplate Mary's unique place in salvation history and then contemplate Mary as a woman among other women. How can Mary's faithfulness be a guide for us? How does her joy in the unknown future help us trust in God's ways? For women, how does she model the need for friends to share in joy and anticipation?

CALLING ALL SINNERS

The Solemnity of All Saints

Readings: Rev 7:2-4, 9-14; Ps 24:1-2, 3-4, 5-6;
1 John 3:1-3; Matt 5:1-12a

"Blessed are the pure in heart, for they will see God." (Matt 5:8)

Apart from brothers and sisters, the most common term the apostle Paul uses to describe his fellow Christians is saints (*hagioi*, "holy ones"). In English, forms of the root *hagi-*, which might appear as nouns, adjectives, or verbs, are translated as "holy," "holy one," "holiness," "sanctification," "sanctified," and "saints." Christians are all saints for Paul: holy ones, set aside for God. Holiness is not something reserved for the special few followers of Christ but is the goal for every Christian, the purpose for which we have been called.

The call for Christians to live up to their baptismal call ought to be a constant reminder that not only are we called to be saints, but we are saints, however imperfectly we are running the race to the heavenly goal. It is not just that we do not share in the eternal joy of heaven now, but that we know how often we fall short of the goal of holiness that Jesus called us to in this life, whether in purity of heart, mercy, righteousness, or peacefulness.

But we have exemplars, for we live in communion with the saints, who share in the fullness of God's life presently. As the *Catechism of the Catholic Church* says, "But at the present time some of his disciples are pilgrims on earth. Others have died and are being purified, while still others are in glory, contemplating 'in full light, God himself triune and one, exactly as he is'" (954). The feast of All Saints is a necessary reminder for us whenever we doubt that God could make a saint of you or me. Sainthood is our purpose and destiny.

Those saints in heaven share the life for which we are being prepared, but they are not simply models for us; they intercede on our behalf. The Revelation of John promises us that the saints are not just a few but a "great crowd" who worship God, calling us home. While the life of the saints is opaque to us in many ways, we have the evidence of Scripture and tradition that it is not just a call to be with God but to be like God. In 1 John, we are told that as saints, "we are God's children now; what we will be has not yet been revealed. What we do know is this: when he is revealed, we will be like him, for we will see him as he is." This is the glorious future, in which some members of the family, children of God like us, already share and in which they mediate for us.

But if we are encouraged to recognize that we are saints even now, how do we make certain we will be saints also then, sharing eternal life with our brothers and sisters in the presence of God, seeing God as God is, like God, for eternity? As with so much of the Christian life, sainthood is a study in the mundane and the ordinary, done with great love of God and neighbor. Jesus, the one and only teacher, instructs us in the Beatitudes, offering us "the paradoxical promises that sustain hope in the midst of tribulations" (*Catechism*, 1717). The paradox, as with so much of the kingdom, is that sainthood confounds and confuses the ways of the world, counseling behavior that others see as foolishness.

Jesus offers that his followers are "blessed" or "happy," which is another suitable translation of *makarios*, when they walk Christ's path of discipleship. In spite of persecution, being reviled, or even mourning, the follower of Jesus is "happy" when showing mercy, making peace, and thirsting for righteousness. This would seem to be a strange definition of "blessed" or "happy." So why are the persecuted, the humble, and the mourning called happy? Part of the reason must be because God is about to reverse this situation: "Rejoice and be glad, for your reward is great in heaven." The "happy" are the saints who are destined for the divine reward, whose lives show that they yearn to share in communion with the saints in heaven.

But to be a saint, as Jesus encourages us, is to live the happy life now, in which virtue allows us to participate in the life of God with joy. Life in the kingdom of God is the goal, but the Beatitudes allow us to participate in that life now with God and all the saints. We are saints, called to be saints, yearning to share in life with the saints.

Life in the presence of God is the goal for which we have been created. Do you see yourself as a saint? How are you able to most fully grasp your sainthood now? What do you most yearn to understand about the life with God and the saints?

Finding a Friend

Second Sunday in Ordinary Time

Readings: 1 Sam 3:3b-10, 19; Ps 40:2, 4, 7-8, 8-9, 10;
1 Cor 6:13c-15a, 17-20; John 1:35-42

"What are you looking for?" (John 1:38)

How do relationships begin? There is naturally not just one way, one place, or one word needed to start a relationship. But is there a common process by which friendship is built from nothing to the point that neither party can imagine life without the other? Some friendships begin in childhood, their origins hazy with time, while others start late in life; but some factors, it seems, are essential to every friendship.

There must be some attentiveness to one's setting to even start a relationship. As a boy, dedicated to the temple in Bethel, Samuel heard the voice of God, but he could not identify it. He thought it was the voice of Eli, the priest to whom his mother Hannah had entrusted him. When he first heard God's voice calling out to him—"Samuel! Samuel!"—he ran to Eli saying, "Here I am!" Samuel mistook God's voice for the voice of Eli two more times. Why did Samuel make this mistake?

It is simple: "Now Samuel did not yet know the Lord, and the word of the Lord had not yet been revealed to him." Attentiveness is essential, but an introduction was needed. Eli, who already had a friendship with God, "perceived that the Lord was calling the boy" after the third time and tells Samuel that when God calls to him again he should say, "Speak, Lord, for your servant is listening." When God called on Samuel a fourth time, he knew he was speaking to God.

Attentive listening is essential to begin any friendship, but an introduction is often necessary, especially to God, whose voice can be mistaken, ignored, or overlooked in a world that values distraction and cacophony over patient listening. An introduction, however, is not enough if there is no openness to begin and maintain a relationship.

We are told that "as Samuel grew up, the Lord was with him and let none of his words fall to the ground." We see this same openness to build a relationship with two of John the Baptist's disciples. John introduced his disciples to Jesus, saying, "Look, here is the Lamb of God!" John's disciples take this introduction as an opportunity to follow after Jesus.

When Jesus saw them following, he asked them a direct question: "What are you looking for?" Their response tells us they were looking for a friend, for they asked Jesus where he was staying. Jesus offered them an open invitation: "Come and see." They accepted the invitation and "remained with him that day." It is time together that creates friendship.

And friendship begets friendship. We see this with Andrew, who was one of John's two disciples. After getting to know Jesus, he returned to tell his brother Simon, proclaiming, "We have found the Messiah." Andrew, who now knew Jesus, needed to share this friendship with his brother. And when Andrew brought Simon to Jesus, Jesus gave him the name Cephas, Aramaic for "rock." Jesus, of course, had intimate knowledge of Simon, for friends give nicknames based on their knowledge of who a person is. Nicknames speak of the love and intimacy that is at the heart of friendship.

Attentiveness, openness, time, and knowledge of each other create and sustain friendships. Paul warns against deceitful intimacy, like that with prostitutes in Corinth, which are based on the use of people. Paul focuses on the harm such false "friendships" create for the individual Christian and for the Body of Christ.

Today we know that such relationships often involve the degradation and even enslavement of those involved in the sex trade, just as they did in Paul's day, when most prostitutes were slaves. No real intimacy or friendship can emerge from the abuse of children, women, or men in such oppressive "relationships." Human relationships, like our relationship with God, must be based on attentiveness to the other and love freely offered. Physical violence and humiliation are at the core of prostitution. They destroy the opportunity for human flourishing, of which genuine friendship is a key element.

There is no substitute in friendship for time; the more time we spend in conversation with God, the more deeply we know God. And the more God's love animates us, the more we are able to offer ourselves to others around us with love. True love makes us unable to accept any other sort of relationship, because to know others deeply is to see God in them and to wish for them the true freedom that comes from being friends of God. We do not want to see them harmed, let alone abused or violated, for a true love of God allows us to see everyone as a neighbor to befriend.

Place yourself with Andrew and Simon. Are you willing to follow and become a friend of Jesus? In terms of your friendships with others, are you allowing true intimacy to grow? How are you seeking the best for your friends and yourself?

FOLLOWING a FrienD

Third Sunday in Ordinary Time

Readings: Jonah 3:1-5, 10; Ps 25:4-5, 6-7, 8-9;
1 Cor 7:29-31; Mark 1:14-20

"Follow me and I will make you fish for people." (Mark 1:17)

When is the best time to repent? Now. Now is the time. Now is always the time. Who knows whether there will be time if you wait? This seems to be the approach of the Ninevites, who appear in the prophetic book of Jonah as the most eager of penitents. Scholars do not see Jonah as a historical account of a mission to Nineveh, but a didactic tale, even a satire, in which irony abounds. It features a recalcitrant prophet, who would rather see the Gentiles properly destroyed than saved, and sailors and denizens of a city noted for its evil and cruelty, who cannot wait to repent of their sins to a God they do not know.

Jonah is notorious for offering the pithiest prophetic message in the Old Testament, only five words in Hebrew: "Forty days more, and Nineveh shall be overthrown!" The same verb used here to describe the coming destruction of Nineveh is used to pronounce the doom of Sodom and Gomorrah in Genesis 19:21, 25 and 29. But its use by Jonah worked on the Ninevites! Upon hearing Jonah's message, the people of Nineveh "believed God; they proclaimed a fast, and everyone, great and small, put on sackcloth." The king of Nineveh becomes a model of true repentance, as he "covered himself with sackcloth, and sat in ashes" and called on his people to "turn from their evil ways and from the violence that is in their hands."

God's gracious response to Nineveh puts Jonah's petulant attitude in perspective: "When God saw what they did, how they turned from their evil ways, God changed his mind about the calamity that he had said he would bring upon them; and he did not do it." It is a humorous story, but it illuminates God's universal compassion and mercy. Forgiveness is a sign of God's power, cast in sharp relief here with the weakness of Jonah's human pettiness.

God's call to repentance in the particular case of Nineveh, however, is a universal call that knows no bounds except the human response: Will we respond when the chance is offered? Paul called the Corinthians to see the world in its eschatological reality, "for the present form of this world is passing away." While the apocalyptic end has not yet arrived, Paul's warning retains its bite today, since all of those whom he first warned in Corinth had to face their own physical deaths. Whether the kingdom comes in power during our lives or we face our physical death as those who came before us did, we must reckon that now is the time of repentance. What other time is there?

Repentance, as the Ninevites demonstrated, is a simple process: turn from sin and turn to God. It is a process of letting go and mourning, like Augustine, the loss of the cruel comfort of sin. But we ought to concentrate more fully on what we gain, namely, a friend who guides us to the highest good, who calls us to the kingdom of God.

Jesus offers this guidance, announcing that "the time is fulfilled, and the kingdom of God has come near; repent, and believe in the good news." It is also personal guidance, for he calls Simon and his brother Andrew as they are "casting a net into the sea . . . And Jesus said to them, 'Follow me and I will make you fish for people.' And immediately they left their nets and followed him. As he went a little farther, he saw James son of Zebedee and his brother John, who were in their boat mending the nets. Immediately he called them; and they left their father Zebedee in the boat with the hired men, and followed him." Repentance here is less about giving up a former life, though it is that, than about gaining a new life with Jesus.

The immediacy of repentance in Mark is also on display, for the new disciples respond without question and follow Jesus. In this way it is no different than the story on display in Jonah when he brings his message to Nineveh. It seems strange, perhaps unbelievable, that people would respond to God so quickly, but there is a reality buttressing these quick decisions. When the truth has been found, and the time is right, why not turn to the truth in fullness? Why not repent now? Why not follow now?

Walk with Jesus along the seashore. What sins must you turn from? What's holding you back? Are you willing to repent and follow Jesus now?

TeLL Me THe GOOD NeWS

Fourth Sunday in Ordinary Time

Readings: Deut 18:15-20; Ps 95:1-2, 6-7, 7-9;
1 Cor 7:32-35; Mark 1:21-28

"What is this? A new teaching—with authority!" (Mark 1:27)

We are all formally students for some time in our lives, and it is best to remain informal students throughout our lives, for there is no point at which there is not something we can learn. At the same time, most of us function as teachers at many points in our lives, some of us professionally but most of us casually, guiding and directing people in ways that might even escape us. We teach by how we live, how we treat people, how we respond under stress, how we reprimand a child, how we help a neighbor, as well as by more concrete and direct ways of teaching.

Some of us, by training and vocation, teach religion and theology, and it is those of us engaged in this vocation who must always remain students in our area of expertise, for Jesus says, "But you are not to be called rabbi, for you have one teacher, and you are all students. And call no one your father on earth, for you have one Father—the one in heaven. Nor are you to be called instructors, for you have one instructor, the Messiah" (Matt 23:8-10). This teaching is directed at all Christians, but it is a difficult teaching for those called upon to be teachers and instructors, for it is easy to forget that in the things of God we are always students.

It is telling, and especially humbling for biblical scholars, to remember that Jesus did not choose his apostles from among the biblical interpreters or experts in Jewish Halakhah (roughly equivalent to canon lawyers today) but from among the fishermen. How could fishermen be teachers in the Bible and Jewish law when they had not been formally trained? What did they know that the experts did not?

What the fishermen knew, or were willing to encounter, was the only true subject: God. The unschooled fishermen knew Jesus, spent time with Jesus, and were willing to learn from Jesus what they did not know. This is why, as Ben F. Meyer wrote years ago, "professional interpreters appear to differ markedly from commonsense readers and, on technical aspects of interpretation . . . they do. In other respects, however, e.g., encounter with the text, report on encounter, critique of truth and value, the superiority of the professionals is random and unreliable" (*Critical Realism and the New Testament* [Eugene, OR: Wipf and Stock, 1989], 28). It was not technical expertise that Jesus sought in his apostles but the willingness to encounter the word of God as life-changing and life-giving.

It was the encounter with truth that led the students, the crowds of ordinary people in Galilee, Judea, and elsewhere, to throng around the teacher Jesus; they responded as people hungry to learn the deepest reality about God and themselves. So, "when the Sabbath came, he entered the synagogue and taught. They were astounded at his teaching, for he taught them as one having authority, and not as the scribes." The religious experts, the scribes, are mentioned, though it seems they are not present, as a contrast to Jesus' authority. Perhaps the experts hung back, wary of how Jesus' teaching might affect their livelihood or authority, or because they disagreed that Jesus' authority was grounded in the Scriptures or God.

Yet, Jesus' final act in the Capernaum synagogue is the demonstration of the divine ground of his teaching authority, for "just then there was in their synagogue a man with an unclean spirit, and he cried out, 'What have you to do with us, Jesus of Nazareth? Have you come to destroy us? I know who you are, the Holy One of God.'" Jesus healed the man of the unclean spirit, and the people were again amazed, referring to this action of Jesus as a "teaching": "They kept on asking one another, 'What is this? A new teaching—with authority!'" It is God's presence and power that is the lesson not only to learn but to encounter.

It is necessary to have teachers in all areas of knowledge, and this includes theology and biblical studies. Expertise and properly ordered authority are essential for all fields. But ultimately we are all students of the one teacher, whose authority is ordered to our salvation and joy. From this school we never graduate; this teacher is always guiding us. This education is perfected for our final purpose: to know God.

Imagine yourself in the Capernaum synagogue. Are you prepared to learn from the one true teacher? What questions do you have for Jesus? What do you still need to learn?

THe WORK OF THe KINGDOM

Fifth Sunday in Ordinary Time

Readings: Job 7:1-4, 6-7; Ps 147:1-2, 3-4, 5-6;
1 Cor 9:16-19, 22-23; Mark 1:29-39

*"Let us go on to the neighboring towns,
so that I may proclaim the message there also."* (Mark 1:38)

Our evaluation of work is equivocal. A person without work is in a precarious situation, financially and emotionally, and being jobless can erode a sense of worth. But those lucky enough to have jobs seem always to be plotting when to retire. Although work is sometimes a burden, it is also necessary. The tension between the need to work and the desire to leave it behind is inherent in the human condition.

The late John Hughes wrote that "human work has been viewed as having a profoundly ambiguous nature throughout the Christian tradition. In the Scriptures apparently differing views lie side by side, and cannot easily be separated. . . . Work in some sense seems to be inseparable from the nature of humanity in its aboriginal goodness, yet this seems not to be necessarily the same as the work that is characterized by toil and struggle" (*The End of Work* [Malden, MA: Blackwell, 2007], 4–5).

Job reflects the relentless toil of human work in his answer to God: "Do not human beings have a hard service on earth, / and are not their days like the days of a laborer?" Job gives voice to the negative sense of work as burden, but though work has a more positive dimension, the Sabbath shows us that work is ultimately relative to what Hughes calls the "higher reality of rest." The true human goal is life in God's rest, yet it seems this too requires some work.

A distinction can be made between the drudgery of daily work and the work for God's kingdom in the New Testament, but it is not the case that we can simply pronounce the work of this world unimportant. There is a goodness that inheres in the work of this world, and we must guard against two distortions of human work: that our work becomes an idol, or that we reject all work to become idle.

Perhaps we can see the goodness of work most fully in evangelization. The apostle Paul had to work in a trade to support himself as a tent-maker, according to Acts 18:3, but it was the work of the Gospel that was most significant for him.

Paul, however, refused to take payment for this work of preaching the Gospel, stating, "If I proclaim the gospel, this gives me no ground for boasting, for an obligation is laid on me, and woe to me if I do not proclaim the gospel! For if I do this of my own will, I have a reward; but if not of my own will, I am entrusted with a commission. What then is my reward? Just this: that in my proclamation I may make the gospel free of charge, so as not to make full use of my rights in the gospel." Paul's work was in the service of the kingdom so that all might enter in and participate in God's eternal rest.

Jesus himself knew the goodness and necessity of work and rest, not just our true goal, to rest in contemplation of God, but in the need to rest from human toil. Jesus' goal on earth was to work for the establishment of the kingdom, and this is why we see his mission in the context of a balance between work and rest. After Jesus heals Peter's mother-in-law in the Gospel of Mark, who resumes her own work of service immediately after she is healed, and after "he cured many who were sick with various diseases, and cast out many demons," he went to seek his own rest in "a deserted place, and there he prayed." Jesus too needed this time of re-creation.

Yet when Peter and the others tracked Jesus down—"hunted for him," says Mark—Jesus did not complain. Jesus responded, "Let us go on to the neighboring towns, so that I may proclaim the message there also; for that is what I came out to do." The New American Bible translation of Mark captures the Greek of this last phrase more closely: "For this purpose have I come." Jesus had work to do and it was essential that it get done.

We ourselves must seek a balance in our own lives, for our work here is necessary and good, but it is not our final purpose. Our final purpose is to enter into the kingdom, so that we might enjoy eternal rest in God's presence.

Travel alongside Jesus in Galilee. Do you value your human work properly? Has it become an idol, too important in your life? Are you setting aside time and ready to work for the Gospel?

THE JOY OF WHOLENESS

Sixth Sunday in Ordinary Time

Readings: Lev 13:12, 44-46; Ps 32:1-2, 5, 11;
1 Cor 10:31–11:1; Mark 1:40-45

"He went out and began to proclaim it freely, and to spread the word."
(Mark 1:45)

In *Impurity and Sin in Ancient Judaism,* Jonathan Klawans outlines the differences between ritual impurity and moral impurity. Moral impurity, which includes acts like adultery and murder, comprises a category of impure, sinful acts. Ritual impurity includes natural processes, like childbirth, marital sexual relations, and menstruation, and does not reflect sinfulness. Leprosy, which designates any number of skin diseases, falls under the category of ritual impurity.

Although a person with a skin disease was guilty of no sin, "he shall remain unclean as long as he has the disease; he is unclean. He shall live alone; his dwelling shall be outside the camp" (Lev 13:46). Someone with leprosy was cut off from the totality of community and religious life. And while most ritual impurities lasted only a short time, often a day or a week, a skin disease could remain with a person in perpetuity.

It is no surprise that when a leper sought out Jesus, he begged him to restore him to physical wholeness so he could live in community again. Kneeling before Jesus, he said simply, "If you choose, you can make me clean." And though he entreated Jesus, he did not plead his case but made a statement of fact: you are able to do this. It was a powerful act of faith in Jesus' power and trust in Jesus' compassion.

Jesus had "pity for the man," rendered by the Greek verb *splanchnizomai,* which indicates deep feelings, affection and love. Jesus was moved by compassion for the leper's situation and "stretched out his hand and touched him." With the word, "Be made clean," and the touch, "immediately the leprosy left him, and he was made clean."

Did Jesus do anything wrong in touching the man? Absolutely not, for although the ritual impurity of a leper was contagious, it was by no means sinful. While Jesus might have made himself technically unclean by touching the man, the healing restored the man immediately, so there was no impurity to transmit. Why does this matter? Because it is important to stress that Jesus was careful to follow the purity laws, not flout them.

After the man was healed, Jesus "sent him away at once, saying to him, 'See that you say nothing to anyone; but go, show yourself to the priest, and offer for your cleansing what Moses commanded, as a testimony to them.'" Jesus' compassion did not spill over into a joyous hug, welcoming the leper back into community; instead, Jesus sent the healed man on his own mission to fulfill the purity laws, as described in Leviticus 14:1-32. The man, by the healing of his leprosy, was only partway to reinstatement in the community. The priest must still examine him, and this process, as outlined in Leviticus, will take over a week to complete. He was on his way to full reintegration in the community, but he was not there yet.

But why did Jesus wish him to "say nothing to anyone"? Did Jesus truly expect this man, joyous at being made whole, to keep quiet? Should he not tell the priests who had healed him? Since Jesus' mission was to call people into the kingdom, why would he tell the newly restored leper to say nothing? The healed leper certainly could not be silent! He "went out and began to proclaim it freely, and to spread the word." The number of people coming to see Jesus increased to such a degree that "Jesus could no longer go into a town openly, but stayed out in the country."

There is tension between Jesus' desire that the leper say nothing and Jesus' mission to proclaim the kingdom. There are a number of statements similar to this in the Gospel of Mark. Scholars call this "the messianic secret" and explore why Jesus calls people to follow him, heals people publicly, and then tells these witnesses to say nothing to anyone. Is this a psychological ploy by Jesus, a literary technique of Mark, a way to keep crowds or authorities from stopping his mission, or a way for Jesus to have his disciples seek for the deeper meaning of what it means to be the Messiah?

Whatever the scholarly answer, the (healed) leper's response suggests that the sheer joy of the Gospel overwhelms those whom Jesus has touched and they cannot keep this joy a secret. Yes, the leper will fulfill the purity laws, but in his gut he knows he cannot remain silent after experiencing the Gospel's healing power. Everyone must know of Jesus' power to heal and restore to wholeness those on the fringes of society.

Envision the scene with the healed leper. How have you experienced and expressed the joy of the Gospel? Are there areas of your life that still need to be restored to wholeness? Have you reached out in prayer to Jesus?

same OLD, same OLD

Seventh Sunday in Ordinary Time

Readings: Isa 43:18-19, 21-22, 24b-25; Ps 41:2-3, 4-5, 13-14;
2 Cor 1:18-22; Mark 2:1-12

*"Do not remember the former things, / or consider the things of old. /
I am about to do a new thing."* (Isa 43:18)

There can be genuine comfort in routine and the habits of daily life—
they fit us like an old, snug sweater and draw us into the rhythms of life.
But there is also the habit of vice and sin, which Augustine described in
Confessions, book VIII, that makes us weary and drowsy, that keeps us
from acting and from changing our ways. This is not just the monotony
of everyday things, or the boredom of a culture overloaded with distract-
ing stimuli; this is the bone weariness of a life weighted with the accumu-
lated sins, mistakes, bad choices, and oppressive situations of many years.
How does one escape from this body of sin?

We can start again! We can write New Year's resolutions! We can go to
confession and promise not to sin again (and mean it!). We can get a new
job, move to a new place, and get some new friends! We can do a spiritual
retreat! We can promise to change our habits, and actually do it! This list,
while not inclusive, is also not meant to be sarcastic or sneering. All of
these things are worthwhile and, at some points in our lives, absolutely
essential. The need to do a searching personal inventory, or a searching
spiritual inventory, is a way to refresh ourselves, combat certain vices or
habits, and take back control of a life stumbling out of control. Still, we
know, if we never, for instance, take a drink again due to the support of
family, friends, AA, and God, there are other issues with which we might
continue to struggle. Starting again never brings us back to square one,
pristine, flawless, and pure.

But that has been the issue from the beginning, ever since the choice
of Adam and Eve and their fall into the slavery of sin. The only plan that
will bring us back to the life for which we were intended is God's plan.

This was inaugurated through the work of Jesus Christ, who as God and man offered himself for the sins of humanity beginning with Adam and Eve. The new start that we all deeply yearn for has begun in God's kingdom, though partially and not yet in full. The apostle Paul speaks of the "yes" that Jesus brings to us as God's promise of life and, more theologically, declares that "it is God who establishes us with you in Christ and has anointed us, by putting his seal on us and giving us his Spirit in our hearts as a first installment."

This seal is the promise of God's ultimate "yes" to humanity and the Holy Spirit is the "first installment" of the new life to come, a new life that brings us back to the Garden, the start and the end. The "first installment" Paul mentions is *arrabōn*, which might also be translated as "guarantee" or "pledge." The working of the Holy Spirit in believers' lives is a taste of the kingdom, the "yes," come to life in our lives, and it also functions as a kind of spiritual "IOU." There is more to come.

One can see the working of God's power as an *arrabōn* in Jesus' own life. Once when Jesus returned to Capernaum a group of friends brought a paralyzed man, and they labored by digging a hole in the roof of the home where Jesus was staying so that their friend could be healed from his paralysis. His illness is a sign of a fallen world, a world in which suffering, corruption, and decay flourish. But Jesus healed the man, a sign of the promise, God's *arrabōn*, that we will have a new start. The healing of the man's paralysis, though, was only a visible sign of the deeper healing Jesus brings, namely, that of our spiritual healing and preparation for the kingdom.

Jesus gave us signs of what the new start would be, and the Holy Spirit confirms for us the newness that has already been inaugurated through Christ's resurrection, but there is more to come. The prophet Isaiah says, "Do not remember the former things, / or consider the things of old. / I am about to do a new thing; / now it springs forth, do you not perceive it? / I will make a way in the wilderness / and rivers in the desert."

Do we perceive it? The new thing is coming, seen imperfectly in our repeated desires to love God, to be more like God, to be transformed spiritually. Do we perceive it? God says in Isaiah, "I, I am He / who blots out your transgressions for my own sake, / and I will not remember your sins." This is not the same old, same old. If it sounds like heaven, that's because it is life with God, a new start that never ends. Something new, God is about to do a new thing.

Think about times in your life when you have tried to change your ways and have stumbled. How did it feel? How did you respond? Think now of times when you were able to change a habit or a situation. How did God work in your life? How did you respond? Do you ever imagine the new start, when God will be all in all, and all things will be new?

A Time To Fast

Eighth Sunday in Ordinary Time

Readings: Hos 2:16b, 17b, 21-22; Ps 103:1-2, 3-4, 8, 10, 12-13;
2 Cor 3:1b-6; Mark 2:18-22

*"The wedding guests cannot fast while the
bridegroom is with them, can they?"* (Mark 2:19)

"Fasting, that is, complete or partial abstinence from nourishment, is an
almost universal phenomenon within both Eastern and Western cultures"
(Rosemary Rader, "Fasting," *Encyclopedia of Religion,* ed. Lindsay Jones
[New York: Macmillan, 2005] 5:2995). There is something profoundly
human about fasting, though it can be difficult often to determine what
the specific purpose is for fasting. In origin, "although it is difficult to
pinpoint a specific rationale or motivation for an individual's or a group's
fasting, in most cultures that ascribe to it at least three motivations are
easily discernible: (1) preliminary to or preparatory for an important event
or time in an individual's or a people's life; (2) as an act of penitence or
purification; or (3) as an act of supplication" (ibid.). We might even want,
in a Christian context, to expand on these motivations, for fasting could
be associated with penance, asceticism, spiritual preparation, purification,
preparation for mystical experience, mourning, supplication, and interior
conversion of heart. What it does not seem to have is a connection to celebration.

This is why Jesus, in response to a question as to why his own disciples
were not fasting, though John the Baptist's disciples and the Pharisees
were fasting, says, "The wedding guests cannot fast while the bridegroom
is with them, can they?" Jesus, by calling himself the bridegroom, is drawing attention to his messianic role during his earthly mission, an image
based on and developed from the notion of God as the bridegroom of
Israel. Yet, even though that earthly mission will end in death for the suffering servant, though of course that is not the end of the story, Jesus is
drawing attention to the fact that when he is with his disciples, mourning
is not the proper orientation. Celebration is the proper state of the bride-

groom and the bride, Jesus' disciples, the church. There is a time for fasting, Jesus says, but this is not the time.

Jesus' ministry was a time of new things, of understanding who he was and of challenging and reinterpreting old paradigms. Change in itself can provoke anxiety and fear, but it is also a time for joy and festivity. It is clear that when Jesus is near, the proper response to him, even in the context of the challenge of new things, is to celebrate a festival. Festivity and challenge give us the context for the sayings on the old and new cloth and the old and new wine.

"No one sews a piece of unshrunk cloth on an old cloak; otherwise, the patch pulls away from it, the new from the old, and a worse tear is made. And no one puts new wine into old wineskins; otherwise, the wine will burst the skins, and the wine is lost, and so are the skins; but one puts new wine into fresh wineskins." A new piece of cloth will shrink as it is washed, pulling away from what is old. New wine, though, can burst the brittle and already stretched wineskins, as it ferments, expands, and bursts its seams. New wine calls for new wineskins.

The metaphor is a fascinating one because of the association of Jesus, the bridegroom, at the wedding at Cana in the Gospel of John. There Jesus produces abundant new wine for the festival, shocking the steward and the guests, since it is better than any wine they had tasted before. At the heart of this wedding feast is celebration and joy. Still, there will be a time for fasting and for Jesus' earthly disciples, when "the bridegroom is taken away from them, and then they will fast on that day." There would be a time for mourning, for penitence, for supplication, for conversion. And that day came. And that day comes for each of us, not just in terms of the church calendar and Lent, but whenever we are far from the bridegroom and need to come closer, whenever we need to turn from sin and renew our relationship with the bridegroom. Whenever we need to draw closer to God.

It does not mean, though, that since Jesus has completed his earthly mission, our days are only to be days of abject sorrow and penitence. We must learn, and relearn, that when the bridegroom is with us, liturgically, in our hearts, in our behavior, in our minds, there is a time to rejoice, to celebrate, and to give thanks. As Jesus said, "As long as they have the bridegroom with them, they cannot fast." We do not always fast because we still have the new wine, the new cloth, the bridegroom who loves us at all times. Yes, there is time to fast, a necessity for our spiritual lives, but because of Christ and what he has done for us, there is always time to celebrate a marriage made on earth and in heaven.

Imagine yourself at a wedding feast. How does Jesus, the bridegroom, draw you to celebration? Where do you experience joy most fully in your spiritual life? When do you need to fast? How do you understand the purpose of fasting in your life?

THe HUMAN TOUCH

Ninth Sunday in Ordinary Time

Readings: Deut 5:12-15; Ps 81:3-4, 5-6, 6-8, 10-11;
2 Cor 4:6-11; Mark 2:23–3:6

"But we have this treasure in clay jars." (2 Cor 4:7)

We are, in Paul's powerful phrase, "clay jars." Clay is prone to breaking and shattering into shards. A malleable material when soft, after firing clay becomes hard and waterproof, but also brittle, susceptible to cracking when dropped or knocked. Many ancient texts were written on potsherds, the remnants of broken clay jars, because the jars once broken were not much good for anything else. And that is what Paul says we are: clay jars.

Like clay jars, human beings are susceptible to cracks and breaking. Unlike clay jars, we are good for more than just bits and scraps. We are fragile vessels that easily crack, but that's the way the light gets in. For Christians the light is due to a perfect offering, though it is not our own perfect offering, but the offering of Christ himself.

It is more than a remarkable piece of metaphor, however, that Paul uses when he calls us "clay jars"; it is a remarkable spiritual insight that God chose flawed and broken human beings to carry the power of God and the message of God to the world. Jesus, the perfect offering, makes us available to carry out tasks beyond our own brittle and broken abilities. Paul seems amazed that God gave to Paul and the other apostles and disciples "this treasure in clay jars," but it is the very fragility of human beings that carries God's word "so that it may be made clear that this extraordinary power belongs to God and does not come from us."

Paul, who will later describe himself as an ambassador for Christ on a mission of reconciliation, notes that all of the suffering he and others undergo for Christ—afflictions, perplexity, and persecutions—are so that Christ might be made known and loved. "For it is the God who said, 'Let light shine out of darkness,'" says Paul, "who has shone in our hearts to give the light of the knowledge of the glory of God in the face of Jesus Christ." Even through our cracks, the light shines on.

But it is also love of humanity that led God to take on the form of broken, clay-like humanity so that he could, ultimately, piece us back together. Though God had reached out through history, giving to stumbling humanity the light of the commandments, as the psalmist says, "But my people did not listen to my voice." The commandments, sometimes misunderstood as burden, were God's gift first to Israel and then the world.

As broken people, we so often turn from God's desires for us, but God's true desire is a humanity that is restored, pieced back together through the perfect offering of the Son, who cares not for laws as such but the restoration of our true destiny. In the grain fields, walking through them with his disciples on a Sabbath, Jesus is challenged by some Pharisees because his disciples are breaking the commandment to keep the Sabbath holy and to do no work on the Sabbath by picking grain. Jesus tells them not only of his authority as Son of Man, but of the purpose of the law: it is for humanity, not against us; it is for our healing, not to burden us.

The next scene in the gospel occurs when Jesus entered the synagogue and encountered a man "who had a withered hand." Some of the religious authorities were on guard to "see whether he would cure him on the sabbath, so that they might accuse him." The point of the law is being missed. The law is for our healing, not our oppression. Jesus healed the man with the withered hand because the deeper principle at work is whether it is "lawful to do good or to do harm on the sabbath, to save life or to kill." God wants to piece us back together, not keep us in our broken state.

Yet, the desire for rigidity in the law and the desire for laxness in the law have the same basic source: that we are clay jars. Sin leads us to expose our fragility and tells us that we can do whatever we choose, exploiting laxness, while rigidity leads us to crack others in our desire to be found worthy. Even as clay jars, though, God has entrusted to us the message of the Gospel, that God has come to us, to put us back together, to heal the cracks, not so that the light cannot come in, but so that we can only carry and emit light.

Imagine yourself as a clay jar, prone to brittleness and breaking. How can you help carry the message of Christ in spite of your brokenness? How does God's trust in us as clay jars demonstrate God's love to you? Where can we let Christ continue to heal our brokenness?

LIFe NOW anD THen

Tenth Sunday in Ordinary Time

Readings: Gen 3:9-15; Ps 130:1-2, 3-4, 5-6, 7-8;
2 Cor 4:13–5:1; Mark 3:20-35

*"We have a building from God, a house not made with hands,
eternal in the heavens."* (2 Cor 5:1)

A challenge of living out our Christian faith is a proper balance of the things of this world and the hope of the world to come. It is not proper to give up on, or to encourage others to give up on, this world, due to our own pain, losses, or even mystical urges, so that we can escape this world and its limitations. On the other hand, it is not proper to think of this world as the end of our lives, but only as the beginning of our lives that are intended to stretch into eternity. That is the balance that must be struck: to live our lives now for the glory of God so that our lives might always continue in the presence of God.

At the beginning of human life, what the Germans call *Urzeit*, the primordial time of humans living in the glory and presence of God, there was no distinction between life on earth and life with God. The two were one. It was sin, the disobedience of human beings, preceded by the disobedience of Satan, which led to the privation of evil from which we all still suffer from today. This "fall" from grace reverberates through the millennia, clouding our judgment, our nature, and our intellect.

It is because of our fall that God came to humanity in the incarnate Word of God, Jesus Christ, sent to rescue us from sin that permeated our existence. What is perhaps most remarkable about Jesus' incarnate life is that people took him at times not to represent God, but evil. On one occasion, Jesus was accused by some scribes from Jerusalem who said, "He has Beelzebul, and by the ruler of the demons he casts out demons." How could this be? How could God with them be identified as a representative of Satan, Beelzebul?

Possibly the scribes are unjustly accusing Jesus, knowing their accusation is untrue, but it is also possible that as representatives of God themselves, they actually believe their accusation. How can Jesus, who has no connections to them, official agents of God, properly know the ways and the word of God? Either scenario points to the insidiousness of sin in human lives. We are fallen, sometimes because we are unable and unwilling to consider the truth of something and sometimes because we desire to cause suffering for someone or gain power for ourselves.

At the beginning, it was not so, for there was only God's presence, only God's love. In this fallen world, however, it is necessary to strive and fight for the truth. All of God's other creations, good in themselves as God's creations, when divorced from their origin and source in God are capable of turning us from the very thing our souls seek: God. This is why Jesus responds as he does when told that "your mother and your brothers and sisters are outside, asking for you." Jesus' reply does relativize family, and all other lower goods, when he says, "Who are my mother and my brothers?" But this relativity is actually essential for our lives to flourish not only in this world but the next, for "whoever does the will of God is my brother and sister and mother."

We need to order our lives to God because when we do we will order our loves here on earth properly and not lose sight of our purposes here or our goal to spend eternity with God. The apostle Paul tells the Corinthians that "we know that the one who raised the Lord Jesus will raise us also with Jesus, and will bring us with you into his presence." That presence Paul yearns for is the reason for Paul's ministry, but it is not just a personal desire; for Paul's whole ministry is based on the goal to bring as many people as possible—everyone!—into God's presence so that they too might share in God's resurrection of Jesus.

The fall of Adam and Eve in the *Urzeit* affected every human being. Heaven, the Garden of Eden, life in the presence of God was intended for the whole human family. So, too, Jesus' conquering of sin and death, thereby opening a path back to God's kingdom, was intended for all humanity. This truth drove Paul's missionary activity and comforted him daily. He writes, "we do not lose heart. Even though our outer nature is wasting away, our inner nature is being renewed day by day. For this slight momentary affliction is preparing us for an eternal weight of glory beyond all measure, because we look not at what can be seen but at what cannot be seen; for what can be seen is temporary, but what cannot be seen is eternal." We are intended for glory, Paul says, for "a house not made with hands, eternal in the heavens." It is the aim of the Christian life, but we return to the home we were intended to inhabit by seeking God's presence now in all we do.

Imagine God's kingdom, heaven, life in the presence of God. How are you preparing for life with God? How are you living your life with God now? How can you help others find their way to God?

THE KINGDOM UNUSUAL

Eleventh Sunday in Ordinary Time

Readings: Ezek 17:22-24; Ps 92:2-3, 13-14, 15-16;
2 Cor 5:6-10; Mark 4:26-34

*"With what can we compare the kingdom of God,
or what parable will we use for it?"* (Mark 4:30)

The first sign that the kingdom of God is not what you expect comes not so much in Jesus' use of parables to describe it but in the content of those parables. Why describe a kingdom by comparing it to the most ordinary of things, like shrubs, seeds, and nesting birds? It is a sign that God is not building a kingdom in line with human expectations. Parables about an ordinary kingdom might focus on the beauty of princesses, the power of warriors, and authority that exalts itself over the weak.

In today's reading from Ezekiel, the prophet also describes in his parable the coming of the unusual kingdom, comparing it to a tree growing from "a sprig / from the lofty top of a cedar." That "sprig" was planted by God on the highest mountain and became "a noble cedar." "Under it every kind of bird will live; / in the shade of its branches will nest / winged creatures of every kind." Jesus reimagines this metaphor, comparing the kingdom of God not to a cedar sprig but to something even more unassuming, a mustard seed, which "when it is sown it grows up and becomes the greatest of all shrubs, and puts forth large branches, so that the birds of the air can make nests in its shade."

Both of these biblical metaphors imagine planting something modest, a shoot or a seed, which grows beyond its inconspicuous beginnings. The cedar gives us a sense of the majesty and nobility of God's unusual kingdom, but the mustard shrub remains ordinary, for even when grown it is only the "greatest of all shrubs," a designation meaningful only to mustard lovers and shrubbery aficionados. But that seems to be Jesus' point.

The growing shrub is not notable for its majesty but for its purpose. And the purpose of the cedar and the mustard shrub is to offer shelter for birds of every kind. What do these birds represent? Biblical scholars agree that the birds represent the nations, the Gentiles, who will find a home in the branches. Though the growth of God's kingdom overwhelms no one, somehow this shrubby kingdom develops to become the home for all people.

But this is not the only metaphor Jesus uses for the kingdom of God, for the kingdom is not simply a shrub waiting for the birds to nest. Jesus uses the parable of the sowing of the seeds to explain how the kingdom is spread to the world. The seeds are scattered over the ground by a sower so that "the seed would sprout and grow, he does not know how." There is a mystery at the heart of the kingdom's growth, here reflected by the unknown growth of the seeds, which stand for the individuals who populate the kingdom.

But just as there is mystery in the sowing and in the growing, there is mystery in the harvesting, for when "the grain is ripe, at once he goes in with his sickle, because the harvest has come." The harvesting is the most mysterious of all the agricultural metaphors of the kingdom of God, for it is our destiny to be cut down. While we grow, struggling to root ourselves, threatened with drought, heat, or other enemies, we are growing to be harvested. Yet our reaping is not our death, for though the kingdom is mysteriously present in us, embodied and alive, the kingdom truly comes when we are "at home with the Lord."

In the parable of the mustard seed, it is clear God has prepared a home for us, which opens itself up to provide shelter and security in its branches for all. Yet God has also planted us and nurtured us to grow for the kingdom of God, a time and a place still to come. But as God has caused the kingdom to grow for us, each of us is also helping the kingdom to grow, providing shelter for others along the way, sowing seeds of love along our own path in the world, the work of the unusual kingdom unknown perhaps to all but God. For the kingdom of God is not the usual game of thrones but a work of love, in which the weak are raised up and the power comes down to earth to live with its subjects, until they are called home to live in the kingdom fully grown.

As you imagine this seemingly unimpressive kingdom of God, what is most impressive about it for you? Where have you seen evidence of the kingdom in the world around you? How have you seen the kingdom of God grow in you and through you?

new creation

Twelfth Sunday in Ordinary Time

Readings: Job 38:1, 8-11; Ps 107:23-24, 25-26, 28-29, 30-31;
2 Cor 5:14-17; Mark 4:35-41

"So if anyone is in Christ, there is a new creation." (2 Cor 5:17)

Even before Darwin, scientists were studying the origin of species; and though some might think there is a perpetual and permanent war between science and religion, it is simply not the case. Saint John Paul II asked in a letter to George V. Coyne, SJ, director of the Vatican Observatory, "If the cosmologies of the ancient Near Eastern world could be purified and assimilated into the first chapters of Genesis, might not contemporary cosmology have something to offer to our reflections upon creation?" (June 1, 1988). While some Christians maintain that the first two chapters of the book of Genesis describe the literal process of creation, most Catholics understand that there is nothing at odds between proclaiming God's sovereignty over creation and studying the means by which creation took place, including the evolution of species.

Yet there is one thing Catholic thought insists on: God is the beginning of all things, the one from whom and through whom all existence emerges. In Job's encounter with God in todays' reading, God challenges Job: "Where were you when I laid the foundation of the earth? / Tell me, if you have understanding. / Who determined its measurements—surely you know! / Or who stretched the line upon it? / On what were its bases sunk, / or who laid its cornerstone . . . Or who shut in the sea with doors / when it burst out from the womb?" The book of Job describes God's creative activity using the language of human building and tools. It is not the scientific reality of these cosmic images that Christians maintain but the insight that we are finite creatures and God is the infinite being, the master builder, who created all out of nothing.

Human beings function as co-creators with God, attempting to understand nature, work with nature, and harness nature. Yet even as human knowledge and technology increase, the tools of human ingenuity are often overwhelmed by the depth of creation, as was Job, not just by how it surprises us with its majesty but because of the limits of our understanding.

For creation is an ongoing work sustained by God. God the creator is not a reminiscence of past events but an affirmation of God as the sustainer of all creation, the one who cares for creation and the one who continues to do new things, even now. God's work in creation is often pronounced in the beauty and power of nature, the vistas of ocean waves, rolling prairies, or soaring mountains. This is the natural world and God is revealed here.

But God's supernatural presence also reveals the God beyond comprehension. The apostles experienced one aspect of God's presence when Jesus, in the midst of a storm, woke to his disciples' anguished cries, "Teacher, do you not care that we are perishing?" Jesus then "woke up and rebuked the wind, and said to the sea, 'Peace! Be still!' Then the wind ceased, and there was a dead calm." The apostles were shocked—an appropriate response, for the might of God rests beyond all human calculation.

And while we might not experience God's supernatural power in a public display that awes us, we might see it worked out at a personal level. Those who have never experienced a natural miracle might experience God working in individual lives, creating something new in people who were lost and forgotten, who were thought beyond redemption. This is why no person is a "loser," no person worthy of being "written off." Cannot the God who creates and sustains all creation, who acts in nature, act in the most precious of creations, human beings? Whenever we cast humanity as masters of the universe, we have lost our way; but whenever we think we are nothing to God, we have misunderstood God's creative power.

God is smaller than that: God dwells in people, working graces unseen. He came to earth out of love and "the love of Christ urges us on, because we are convinced that one has died for all." Each of us is a miracle not only in the womb but at every stage of our lives. This is why Paul says, "So if anyone is in Christ, there is a new creation: everything old has passed away; see, everything has become new!" We are new creations, for God is working in each of our lives even now. The Creator beyond all human imagining loved us into being and makes each of us new.

Consider the transcendence and immanence of God. When you consider God, what is most amazing to you? When you consider God's creation, what moves you most profoundly? In what way has God been making a new creation in you?

NO DELIGHT IN DEATH

Thirteenth Sunday in Ordinary Time

Readings: Wis 1:13-15; 2:23-24; Ps 30:2, 4, 5-6, 11, 12, 13; 2 Cor 8:7, 9, 13-15; Mark 5:21-43

"God did not make death, / and he does not delight in the death of the living." (Wis 1:13)

God is for us and for life. God, after all, "did not make death, / and he does not delight in the death of the living." Death is our enemy, and God has joined with us to battle against it. The Gospel of Mark invites us to see how God is fighting for us through the stories of a Jewish woman and a Jewish girl on the cusp of maturity.

Jairus is a leader in the synagogue and his daughter is near death. He acknowledges Jesus' power over death by falling at his feet and begging him "repeatedly" to come and heal his child. Jairus had faith that Jesus could heal his daughter: "My little daughter is at the point of death. Come and lay your hands on her, so that she may be made well, and live." Jesus responds to his appeals and follows him.

As he is leaving, though, a woman in the crowd waylays him. She "had been suffering from hemorrhages for twelve years." Like Jairus, she was desperate; and her scene now comes into the foreground, leaving Jairus and his ailing daughter in the background.

Mark uses this technique often in his gospel. He cuts away from a scene, introduces another scene, and then completes the first scene. Biblical scholars call this a "sandwich technique," with the two stories offering clues as to how to interpret each in light of the other. The story of Jairus and his daughter is not being abandoned; indeed, the woman with a hemorrhage will help us more fully understand it.

Jesus immediately responds to the suffering woman's entreaty, for the moment she touches him she is made well, and though a crowd is pushing against Jesus, he senses the power of her faith, which elicited the healing. When Jesus asks, "Who touched me?" she acknowledges that it was she and, like Jairus, "fell down before him." Jesus says, "Daughter, your faith has made you well; go in peace, and be healed of your disease."

As her story ends, some members of Jairus's house come to tell him to send Jesus away because another daughter, his daughter, has died. Jesus overhears the conversation, though, and tells them, "Do not fear, only believe" (5:36). The translation of the verb *pisteuo* as "believe" is misleading, though, for it has the same root as the noun for "faith," *pistis*, just used earlier with the woman with a hemorrhage. The verb should be translated "only have faith." Jesus is asking Jairus to maintain the faith he had when he fell before Jesus and begged him to help, the same faith the woman had just shown when she was healed. But Jairus's daughter is not merely bleeding, she is dead. What faith is sufficient over death?

When Jesus arrives at Jairus's home, people are understandably crying and wailing loudly at the death of the girl. Jesus appears almost to be mocking them when he asks the people why they are crying and claims, "The child is not dead but sleeping." The people laugh at him, but Jesus puts everyone except the girl's parents and three apostles out of the house. He grasps the dead girl's hand and speaks to her in Aramaic, *Talitha cum*, which means, "Little girl, get up!" The girl, who we are now told is twelve years old, does get up and begins to walk.

The woman healed and the girl raised have some things in common: They are female; they are both called daughter; and they are linked by the number twelve. The number is a sign of the restoration of the twelve tribes of Israel at the end of time, a sign of the Messiah and the eschaton. Israel is also known as the daughter or even the bride of God (Hos 2:19-21). In these healings, Jesus shows that he has come to bring daughter Israel to health and full life.

The healings that connect these daughters of Israel are signs of the spiritual wholeness and the destruction of death that the Messiah brings. And since we know that God "does not delight in the death of the living," we know that new life for the restored people of Israel was a sign of the offer extended to the whole world. Wherever death comes to destroy, faith in Christ's healing power is sufficient, even over death.

Reflect on this girl and this woman. How has death impacted your own life? How does this account of Jesus' raising up the girl to new life inspire hope in you? How has God restored life in you?

Transformed by the Messiah

Fourteenth Sunday in Ordinary Time

Readings: Ezek 2:2-5; Ps 123:1-2, 2, 3-4;
2 Cor 12:7-10; Mark 6:1-6

"Whenever I am weak, then I am strong." (2 Cor 12:10)

If you want to be transformed by the Messiah, the first step is to recognize the Messiah in your midst. This means being ready to encounter the Son of God wherever you are and whatever time it is. This means inclining not just your ear for God's voice, but your heart for God's presence.

During the time of the prophet Ezekiel, God spoke to him, saying, "I am sending you to the people of Israel, to a nation of rebels who have rebelled against me; they and their ancestors have transgressed against me to this very day." God claimed the people were "impudent and stubborn" but that they would know that a prophet had been sent to them, if not when the call of repentance was given, then sometime in the future.

But hard hearts and crooked ways are not just something in the past. What Ezekiel found in his own day is precisely what we find today in our own hearts. Will we listen, hear, and do what is necessary when God speaks?

An essential aspect to both hearing God and then doing God's will is humility, for often God is speaking to us things we do not want to hear and telling us things we would rather not do. Jesus in his own hometown faced a lack of humility, with people unwilling to open themselves up to the will of God. Mark tells us that Jesus "could do no deed of power there, except that he laid his hands on a few sick people and cured them." The reason for this was their "unbelief," which in Greek is *apistia*, "lack of faith." What Jesus explains as "lack of faith" might also be described as unwillingness to acknowledge God's will and then to cooperate with it. If we refuse to respond, there is little God can do.

The apostle Paul offers us another picture, that of a man convinced he was doing God's will when he persecuted the earliest disciples of Jesus, acting as a man of violence and anger to impose his will on a way he did not understand. But when Saul was struck by the presence of the risen Jesus, he changed his ways. As stunning as his encounter with the risen Lord was, it was still incumbent on Paul to acknowledge it was the Lord and to radically change his own ways.

And what changed most profoundly with Paul was his humility, his willingness to repent of his past persecutions and to admit to a past that shamed him. The genuineness of his humility is seen most clearly in his readiness to go from persecutor to persecuted, to suffer all things for the word of God. For in light of the crucified one, life was no longer about imposing Paul's will. It was about hearing and following the will of God, whose Son had transformed him.

Jesus told Paul in the context of one of his revelations, "My grace is sufficient for you, for power is made perfect in weakness." Each of these claims, however, required sacrifice on the part of Paul: to accept God's grace is to let go of our own ways and desires; to believe that power is made perfect in weakness is to accept that we are indeed weak and powerless. This means listening for God but also doing what God desires even when we would rather not follow.

What is more is that Paul heard God's call, accepted God's grace, and lived out God's powerful weakness in his own life. For though Paul experienced these overwhelming revelations of God's radiant presence, of the voice of God speaking to him, he was willing to be "content with weaknesses, insults, hardships, persecutions, and calamities for the sake of Christ."

We too, even today, can experience the risen Lord in our midst if we attend to him, even if our experiences are not as overwhelming as Paul's conversion or subsequent revelations. We too, still today, are called to be open to God's word and to hear it. We too must have faith no matter the circumstances in which we are called, or to what we are called, even though we might prefer an easier path. For in our humility comes our transformation to greatness in imitation of our Lord: "for whenever I am weak, then I am strong."

Place yourself with Jesus on his return to his hometown. Are you willing to be transformed by Christ in your midst? Are you willing to listen to things that challenge your way of life? Are you open to humility?

WHere DO YOU LIVe?

Fifteenth Sunday in Ordinary Time

Readings: Amos 7:12-15; Ps 85:9-10, 11-12, 13-14;
Eph 1:3-14; Mark 6:7-13

"Wherever you enter a house, stay there until you leave." (Mark 6:10)

Jesus sends (*apostellō*) his messengers (*apostoloi*) out into the world to share his message and his ministry, but the sending of the apostles is not so much about traveling vast distances as it is about being present for the people around them. Wherever you live, that is the place evangelization occurs.

Jesus stresses this aspect of presence when he says, "Wherever you enter a house, stay there until you leave." A word missing from this translation (NRSV) is the Greek adverb *ekeithen*, "from that place." As a whole the sentence would read, "Wherever you enter a house, stay there until you leave from that place," indicating presence in the place where you are. We are to be grounded to a place, which today we might call inculturation.

In Canada, First Nations people today are dealing with the aftermath of residential schools, in which a number of Christian churches contracted to run schools on behalf of the government of Canada. Such schools, instead of being sources of Gospel presence, were often places of sexual, physical, and emotional abuse and even death. They were also called by Judge Murray Sinclair, the chair of Canada's Truth and Reconciliation Commission, a source of "cultural genocide." The former prime minister of Canada, Stephen Harper, apologized for the residential schools in 2008, as did the United Church of Canada, the Anglican Church of Canada, the Presbyterian Church of Canada, and various groups within the Roman Catholic Church of Canada at earlier dates. Much still remains not just to be said, but to be done.

But how could evangelization turn so foul and lead to abject cruelty in so many cases? A large part of the sinfulness had to do with not respecting the inherent dignity of native peoples and not living with them in their place, but attempting to turn the Gospel into a particular instantiation of

European Christianity. Pope Francis reminds us in The Joy of the Gospel (2013) that "the mere fact that some people are born in places with fewer resources or less development does not justify the fact that they are living with less dignity" (*Evangelii Gaudium* 190).

Jesus sent his apostles to live with people as they were and where they were, and to invite them to live with him. Indeed, when two disciples of John the Baptist encountered Jesus, they did not ask him, "Who are you?" but "Where are you staying?" Jesus told them to "come and see," and they remained with Jesus that whole day (John 1:38-39).

It is the encounter and dwelling with Jesus that creates disciples. The apostles are able to represent Jesus because they know him and have lived with him. Just as he welcomed them, they are to welcome and stay with all they meet, relying not on material goods but on God and the kindness of strangers.

A part of their evangelistic proclamation of the coming of God's kingdom is the call "that all should repent." Embedded in the call, though, is the cost of rejection. Those who hear the message and reject it bear a burden, but it is a burden that weighs especially heavily on those who have been commissioned to proclaim the message but refuse to live it. We all need to hear the message anew and to be prepared always to repent, for "the Church does not evangelize unless she constantly lets herself be evangelized" (*Evangelii Gaudium* 174).

What is amazing is how many First Nations people heard the Gospel message in spite of its flawed and sinful bearers, in spite of the cruelty inflicted on their people and their culture. This is because the Gospel, when encountered in its joyous truth, reveals "a single home" for all people in the church to dwell (On Christian Joy, Pope Paul VI, 1975). This "single home" must always be ready to welcome strangers into the family.

Even more, we must be able to repent when the Gospel of joy and hospitality has been tarnished with the cruelty of racism and prejudice. When we bring the Gospel, it must be with a spirit of humility. If we are asking people to stay with us in our single home, we must be willing to remain with them, where they are, and recognize that God dwells with them too.

Be with Jesus where you live. How are you evangelizing for the kingdom? Have you confronted racism and prejudice in your community or in your own life? Are you willing to live and offer the Gospel in humility?

SHePHerD US

Sixteenth Sunday in Ordinary Time

Readings: Jer 23:1-6; Ps 23:1-3, 3-4, 5, 6;
Eph 2:13-18; Mark 6:30-34

"I will raise up shepherds over them who will shepherd them."
(Jer 23:4)

The problem is not a new one among the flocks of the Lord. The prophet Jeremiah sounded a warning over twenty-five hundred years ago, chastening those who would mislead the sheep: "Woe to the shepherds who destroy and scatter the sheep of my pasture! says the LORD." It is also a current problem, as a priest at the parish my family attended for over ten years was recently jailed for sexual abuse of minor boys. The lack of oversight by the shepherds of the archdiocese was laid bare in the local and national media for all to see. It is a reality that drives people out of parishes, and even from the church.

Each of us is responsible before God for our behavior, but those who have been assigned to care for the people of God, the shepherds who have been asked to guide the sheep, have a heavy burden when the sheep are scattered and driven away due to the actions, or lack of action, by the shepherds. God chastises the shepherds "who have scattered my flock, and have driven them away."

Through Jeremiah, God promised that the scattered "remnant of my flock" would be gathered up and good shepherds raised up to guide them. While the historical context of the Babylonian exile is clear in these promises to Israel through the prophet Jeremiah, the eschatological context is also evident in God's promise to "raise up for David a righteous Branch," who would "reign as king and deal wisely." This promised Messiah was raised up as the Good Shepherd not just for the people of Israel, but also for all of the sheep who did not belong to that one fold (John 10:16).

And it was through the life of the Good Shepherd that we "who once were far off have been brought near by the blood of Christ." The shepherd not only protected his sheep, but gave up his own life to bring us to life eternal. This compassion for the flock, both those who knew the voice of the shepherd and those who were not yet aware of their heritage as God's people, enlivened all that Jesus did in his mission. His work was for the life of his flock.

Jesus also raised up shepherds to continue to guide the flock. After being sent out to evangelize, the apostles reported back to Jesus on everything "they had done and taught." The Good Shepherd's compassion extended to these protégés, whom Jesus knew needed rest, so he took them to a deserted place. But though they "went away in the boat to a deserted place by themselves," they could not find much time alone, for the people had already tracked them down and discerned the place they were going, waiting there when the disciples arrived.

Yet Jesus, when he "saw a great crowd," did not turn from the flock and focus on the shepherds. Jesus' compassion was poured out on the sheep "because they were like sheep without a shepherd." Jesus' compassion instead was a model for the shepherds who would continue his mission. In responding to the needs of the flock, Jesus gives us the priorities of the Good Shepherd: serve the people; care for the people; build up the people. These are the priorities not just of the Good Shepherd; they must be the priorities also of the successors to the apostles, who have been called to shepherd the people.

There are no excuses for shepherds who scatter the flock and drive people away. It is not that there is not forgiveness from God for all those who repent, for sin stalks all of the sheep of the flock. But when shepherds are unable to bear the burden of caring for the sheep, protecting the sheep, and even aid in the destruction of the sheep, they will indeed be forgiven when they genuinely repent. Still, even with forgiveness, they must never be allowed to guard the sheep any longer. It is for this reason that Pope Francis has recently established tribunals to deliberate on negligence among bishops.

All of us stumble, but true shepherds do not repeatedly put the sheep, especially the little ones, in harm's way, time after time, year after year, and then claim to be doing the work of the Lord. The Good Shepherd gave himself up for the sheep; woe to those shepherds who give up the sheep to protect themselves.

Have you or your parish been impacted by the sexual abuse crisis or some other scandal? How has it affected you or those you know and their attitudes to the church? What changes do you think the church should make in response to this crisis? Pray for your shepherds that they model themselves on the Good Shepherd.

No one SHOULD Have NOTHING

Seventeenth Sunday in Ordinary Time

Readings: 2 Kgs 4:42-44; Ps 145:10-11, 15-16, 17-18;
Eph 4:1-6; John 6:1-15

"Where are we to buy bread for these people to eat?" (John 6:5)

A couple of days before the release of Pope Francis's encyclical *Laudato Sì*, a neighbor and I were discussing rumors about the encyclical and what it might contain concerning the state of the earth and economic systems. It was an intriguing conversation, because my neighbor does not identify as a Christian, or even a theist, but his concern for the needs of humanity and the earth is evident in how he lives. We were discussing the need for all people to have food, clothing, education, a home, and all other basic necessities, when I noted that there would never be genuine equality among people with respect to money and goods because of a variety of factors, including talent, skill, and even luck.

It was then that he said, "But no one should have nothing." That cut to the heart of the matter. All of us as God's precious creations deserve in this world the basic necessities. And there is enough. In fact, with God in our sights, there is always some left over.

There is a story in the Second Book of Kings, a story that Christopher T. Begg says "is obviously the inspiration for New Testament multiplication miracles" ("1–2 Kings," in *The New Jerome Biblical Commentary*, ed. Brown, Fitzmyer, and Murphy [Englewood Cliffs, NJ: Prentice Hall, 1990], 176), in which Elisha is given the firstfruits of the harvest as a "man of God." Most Old Testament traditions see these firstfruits as offered to the official representatives of the temple, the priests and Levites, or to the temple itself, the house of God (e.g., Exod 23:19; Lev 23:10), but all of the firstfruits are truly an offering to God through the representatives of God, which Elisha the prophet really is.

Elisha does not keep the firstfruits offering for himself, however, but offers it to the people, saying, "Give it to the people and let them eat."

Elisha's servant complains that the twenty barley loaves will never feed one hundred people, but Elisha reiterates that God had said, "They shall eat and have some left." What Elisha received as a representative of God, he gave back to the people. Everyone ate, as promised, and there was some left over.

Jesus' teaching on the multiplication of the loaves and fishes starts with human need too, in which the few fish and loaves of a little boy became an outpouring of food for the gathered crowd. Jesus, says the Gospel of John, knew what his plan was, but he asked his apostle Phillip, "Where are we to buy bread for these people to eat?" "Philip answered him, 'Six months' wages would not buy enough bread for each of them to get a little.'" Jesus then took the five barley loaves and two fish and fed five thousand people, with twelve baskets full left over.

There is no question that Jesus' actions and the stories that recount them, found in all four gospels, are modeled on the account of Elisha feeding a hungry crowd. There is also no question that in both stories there is a spiritual meaning that runs deeper than the simple physical act of nourishing the body. Elisha gives the people the food dedicated to God as the firstfruits; Jesus will offer himself, the "first fruits of those who have died" (1 Cor 15:20), as the spiritual bread from heaven. But the spiritual truth does not negate the meaning of the material bread and the necessary sustenance it offers.

It was the miraculous act of multiplication that drew the people to Jesus, says John, that made them want "by force to make him king" and led them to proclaim, "This is indeed the prophet who is to come into the world." But it is the act of giving what is needed physically that allows people to see with the eyes of the soul, to look beyond this world to the world eternal, from the barley bread to the bread of heaven. God's abundance, poured out over the whole earth, is intended for everyone. All are called to participate in this richness, to be a part of the one body and one Spirit, sharing in the material and the spiritual bread.

This is not Elisha or Jesus teaching lessons in economics but lessons in theology, the nature of God's ways. If our economics does not make room for feeding everyone, with some left over, it is not because the church's science is faulty but because of our hardened hearts. There is enough for everyone, and no one should have nothing.

Reflect on the crowds around Jesus. How have you responded to the material needs of people? How has your church shared its goods with the people of your community? What can you share from the abundance you have received?

HUNGER FOR THE TRUTH

Eighteenth Sunday in Ordinary Time

Readings: Exod 16:2-4, 12-15; Ps 78:3-4, 23-24, 25, 54;
Eph 4:17, 20-24; John 6:24-35

"I am the bread of life. Whoever comes to me will never be hungry."
(John 6:35)

There is a fine line between having what we need to sustain our physical existence and feeling we just do not have enough. Or is that line the one where we want more and more? Once we cross that line, as individuals and as societies, to where our most notable identification is as a consumer, it can be difficult to cross back. Once this takes place, the most surprising of things begins to happen: Our own sense of worth and value can be tied up in things we own and things we buy. Even sadder, though this is sad enough, we begin to see other people as valuable on the basis of their power to buy things and accumulate "stuff." Poor people themselves become less valuable, and all kinds of ways are concocted to explain how they are responsible for being poor and the architects of their own fate.

For many of us in the West, myself included, food is something of which we consume too much and waste too often, while many others suffer with too little. Part of having more than enough is being thankful for the abundance and properly stewarding what is left over. The Israelites knew what it was to be bereft and called out to God to supply their needs. God did it, but it was also a test, to see "whether they will follow my instruction or not." God provided for their physical needs: "he rained down on them manna to eat, / and gave them the grain of heaven. / Mortals ate of the bread of angels; / he sent them food in abundance." But the test was a spiritual one, and it is one that each wealthy nation and person must take today: How are we handling our abundance?

Jesus challenged those who followed him after the multiplication of loaves and fishes to take the same test. He asked the crowds, who continued to follow him, if "you are looking for me, not because you saw signs, but because you ate your fill of the loaves." Because the human needs are so real and genuine, it can be easy to focus on them when they are met and to see physical needs as the goal of life. Jesus asks his followers to look beyond and not to "work for the food that perishes, but for the food that endures for eternal life, which the Son of Man will give you." It is only the spiritual food that will satisfy our deepest needs.

It is a properly ordered life that assigns to all human needs their right place. The author of Ephesians, traditionally understood to be the apostle Paul, challenges us to take this test and not to abandon ourselves "to licentiousness [*aselgeia*], greedy to practice every kind of impurity [*akatharsia*]. . . . You were taught to put away your former way of life, your old self, corrupt and deluded by its lusts [*epithymia*], and to be renewed in the spirit of your minds." The prominent concern in this passage is with sexual licentiousness, but sexual lust is not the only desire that can lead us astray. Unbridled passions can consume every area of our lives, corrupting and deluding us.

Aselgeia, *akatharsia*, and *epithymia* can also reflect other disordered desires, whether for too much food, bigger houses, or more cars. Social sins, of course, can be the hardest to see, because the way a society lives can come to seem the normal, the best, even the only way to live. While we might ask how people lived justifying the evils of slavery, we must ask ourselves how we live justifying the evils of overconsumption. How do we justify overuse of food and other natural resources, throwing away tons of food daily, while others go without basic needs being met?

Ephesians asks us "to be renewed in the spirit of your minds." This is not a renewal of ideological purity, of the right or the left, of this political party or that, but a renewal in the spirit of God's Word, the Word made flesh. This renewal criticizes every human vanity and every form of human impurity; it strips excuses away and leaves us hungry for the truth alone.

This is the hunger that compels us to demand, "Sir, give us this bread always." Jesus tells us, "I am the bread of life. Whoever comes to me will never be hungry, and whoever believes in me will never be thirsty." It is this bread that orders all our appetites and allows us to turn away from the desires of selfishness and indifference so that we can clothe ourselves "with the new self, created according to the likeness of God in true righteousness and holiness."

Listen to Jesus speak to the crowd. Are your material needs being met? How are you utilizing your abundance of food and other goods? Are your ultimate desires ordered to the bread of heaven?

A SENSE OF GOD

Nineteenth Sunday in Ordinary Time

Readings: 1 Kgs 19:4-8; Ps 34:2-3, 4-5, 6-7, 8-9;
Eph 4:30–5:2; John 6:41-51

"O taste and see that the LORD is good." (Ps 34:8)

As infants, prior to the coming of speech, we communicate with sounds, gestures, and facial expressions. Long before we can speak to our mothers, fathers, or older siblings, we fall in love with them. It is a tactile love, based upon the senses of touch, hearing, smelling, and seeing. What if this is how we fall in love with God?

These sorts of tactile images abound in Scripture, in which the physical senses are used to describe our relationship with God. Theologians refer to these descriptions as "spiritual senses." Spiritual senses are not always used in the Bible as a metaphor, they argue, but analogically as a way to describe how we discern the presence of God, actual spiritual senses by which we communicate and enter into relationship with God.

In the modern period Augustin-Francois Poulain, SJ, in *The Graces of Interior Prayer*, stated that "the words to see God, to hear and to touch him are not mere metaphors. They express something more: some close analogy" ([St. Louis, MO: Herder, 1950], 90). Poulain would argue that there are passages in the Bible where the senses that describe our ability to touch, taste, hear, smell, and see God are not merely metaphors, but actually describe a sensory relationship with God, albeit spiritual. So, when the psalmist asks us to "taste and see that the LORD is good," there is a spiritual sense to which the image refers that is not exhausted by a metaphor that evokes a remembrance of a wonderful meal or even physical participation in the eucharistic feast.

But the connection between the physical senses and the spiritual senses is always present, for the physical senses are the means by which we become sensitive to spiritual realities and grounded in the reality of God's presence. The story of Elijah in the First Book of Kings brings to bear these physical and spiritual senses, for Elijah is running from physical danger, a threat to his life by Jezebel, to Mount Horeb, the place where Moses experienced the theophany, the presence of God. It is there that Elijah will experience God's presence in the silence, hear God's voice and speak with him.

Before arriving at Mount Horeb, though, Elijah "asked that he might die," because of the threats on his life and the belief that he had failed at his task. Instead, as Elijah was sleeping an angel "touched him, and said, 'Get up and eat.'" Twice the angel did this before Elijah ate the cake and drank the water supplied for him by God's messenger. It was only after this physical sustenance that Elijah traveled forty days and forty nights to receive the revelation of God, to experience the presence of the divine.

These mystical experiences might seem merely a product of ancient imagination or to be linked only to holy figures of the past, but it seems that the key to encountering God in our own lives is to be able to look beyond the physical realities, essential not only to our bodies but to our growth as spiritual beings, and to feel God's presence. To become awakened to the reality of the spiritual senses in our lives is to discern God among us.

In the Letter to the Ephesians, the author asks that we "be imitators of God, as beloved children, and live in love, as Christ loved us and gave himself up for us, a fragrant offering and sacrifice to God." This is the only place in all of the New Testament where we are asked to imitate God; this is probably due to the focus in Ephesians on God as father. Children in antiquity were to form themselves in the image of their father. This, of course, had its practical realities; but more significantly, imitation had spiritual dimensions. How are we to imitate God unless we have come to know God intimately, as a child knows his or her parents?

Imitation of God is grounded in love of the Father who gave his Son for us as "a fragrant offering and sacrifice to God," and as "the bread that came down from heaven." But to smell the fragrant offering and to taste the heavenly bread propels us to senses beyond the physical. These senses offer up for us a world in which we are able to "taste and see that the LORD is good."

Picture the spiritual senses. Does the notion of spiritual senses enlighten your understanding of the spiritual life? Have you ever experienced God through a spiritual sense? What spiritual sense describes most fully how you enter into relationship with God?

FOOD OF WISDOM

Twentieth Sunday in Ordinary Time

Readings: Prov 9:1-6; Ps 34:2-3, 4-5, 6-7;
Eph 5:15-20; John 6:51-58

"Come, eat of my bread / and drink of the wine I have mixed."
(Prov 9:5)

You are what you eat. There is some truth to this in the physical sense, as the bloated Western diet can lead us to heart disease and obesity, while more nutritious and moderate eating can lead to better health and more energy. Yet every physical food, in moderation, can be transformed into necessary fuel for the body.

But it is certainly true that in the spiritual sense, we are what we eat. What you eat is what you get. If you want wisdom, you need to partake of wisdom; for foolishness, unlike junk food, cannot be transformed into an essential component of the spiritual self. Even more, when you taste wisdom, there is no limit to the amount you can eat. It fills you up but always leaves you wanting more.

Proverbs bids us to eat of the spiritual food of wisdom. In vivid and evocative language, promising that "she has slaughtered her animals, she has mixed her wine, / she has also set her table," Wisdom says, "Come, eat of my bread / and drink of the wine I have mixed."

There is an analogic sense to eating and drinking in wisdom, for as with physical food, we come to know the best food by growing it, cooking it, and tasting it. The more we try certain foods or types of wine, the more we know what is best. It is a matter of developing our palates, becoming sensitive to the food we eat, refining our tastes, and discerning what is most healthy and nutritious.

There is no difference with the spiritual sense of food. To eat of wisdom is to "walk in the way of insight," says Proverbs, while foolishness is "immaturity." Wisdom is a spiritual food, and you need to become a gourmand. You need to know how to source it, to find the best purveyors, to find the hidden gems.

The call in the Letter to the Ephesians that we live "not as unwise people but as wise" is a call, therefore, to be discerning in the spiritual food we eat. We are told to "not be foolish, but understand what the will of the Lord is." This is the process of a discerning palate, as eating at the table of wisdom is a process of insight and habituation, as is any growth in virtue. When we recognize that true spiritual food is what allows us to grow in wisdom, it becomes the only food we want to eat. The Alexandrian theologian Origen said that the spiritual sense of taste "feeds on living bread that has come down from heaven and gives life to the world" (*De Principiis* I.1.9). Participating in this meal is the height of wisdom.

Here we eat the meal that embodies wisdom itself, but only if our spiritual senses are attuned to the reality of this food. The dispute that Jesus' teaching engenders in the Gospel of John, when some ask, "How can this man give us his flesh to eat?" is a good question when based on the physical senses. Christ's flesh is truly being consumed, but it is spiritual wisdom that opens our eyes to the reality of the meal that goes beyond the physical elements. "My flesh is true food and my blood is true drink," but only for those who have the ability to see that it is the spiritual food designed to bring us to eternal life.

If one does not discern the spiritual reality behind the claim "unless you eat the flesh of the Son of Man and drink his blood, you have no life in you," it will simply be misunderstood as a physical impossibility or foolishness.

And it is only by eating at the table of wisdom in all its forms that deeper spiritual realities come to be understood. We need to taste and see all that wisdom offers us, for only when we have been trained and had our palates refined can we understand what it means to eat from the table of wisdom. Wisdom lays out a table for each of us every day, in the course of our work, with our families at home, and even at play and at leisure. We need to be able to pick and choose from the table of wisdom, for the more we taste of it, the more discerning we become, until the only food we desire is wisdom itself, embodied in the Body and Blood of Christ at the eucharistic table.

Contemplate the nature of wisdom. What are your sources for wisdom? What has allowed you to discern true wisdom? On a daily basis, how are you eating and drinking in wisdom?

SUBJECTS, NOT OBJECTS

Twenty-First Sunday in Ordinary Time

Readings: Josh 24:1-2a, 15-17, 18b; Ps 34:2-3, 16-17, 18-19, 20-21;
Eph 5:21-32; John 6:60-69

"Be subject to one another out of reverence for Christ." (Eph 5:21)

Ancient Roman society was profoundly hierarchical, and this can grate on readers today when they encounter certain biblical passages. Prime among these are ancient household codes, which delineate the duties and responsibilities of family members to one another. Part of the purpose of these passages in their historical context was to show how Christians fit within ancient Roman society.

Margaret Y. MacDonald, one of the preeminent interpreters of the household codes today, writes in her book *The Power of Children* about how "discussion of the apologetic functions of the New Testament household codes has frequently led to consideration of how the codes may be framing messages intended to be communicated directly or indirectly to the neighbors of believers who are wondering what exactly is going on in these household cells." But she goes on to say that "what is emerging especially clearly is not simply the accommodating nature of the household codes, but elements of resistance that stand out more sharply when ideological correlations are noted" (Waco, TX: Baylor, 2014; p. 105).

The "elements of resistance" in the Letter to the Ephesians are grounded in the family's allegiance to Christ above allegiance to the Roman emperor, for subjection to one another is "out of reverence for Christ," not out of concern for the good order of the empire. Christians certainly wanted to make clear that they did not intend to subvert the basic harmony of Rome; but the fact that their family life was based in obedience to Christ, the true Lord, did indeed manifest an element of subversion.

The second "element of resistance" in Ephesians, however, has to do with the relationship of wife to husband. On the surface, the teaching in Ephesians promotes the basic hierarchical relationship between husbands and wives in the ancient Roman Empire: "Wives, be subject to your husbands as you are to the Lord. For the husband is the head of the wife." Some Christians read the passage today as a statement about a wife's inferiority and subordination to her husband. But this passage calls husbands and wives to "be subject to one another out of reverence for Christ." The passage is not about the objectification of women.

Ephesians cites Genesis 2:24 when it speaks of the unity of husband and wife. Recall that when Jesus spoke of marriage in Matthew 19:4 and 8, he too cited Genesis, proclaiming that unity was intended "at the beginning" of creation for male and female. Yet Jesus' teaching applies not only to divorce but to the wholeness and oneness their primal relationship was intended to celebrate. The unity of man and woman that God established in the Garden was not marked by domination and objectification but by mutuality.

Reflect on Christ, the letter says, as the example for husbands to "love your wives, just as Christ loved the church and gave himself up for her." The husband's model is the *kenosis*, the self-emptying, of Christ for the church. And wives are to "be subject to your husbands as you are to the Lord." But subjection to Christ is subjection to the one who offers himself for us, who loves us until death. This is marriage as idealized through Christ, but in neither element of this relationship is there room for objectification of the other or claims of superiority, since we are called to "be subject to one another out of reverence for Christ." True relationships never serve brutish whims.

This is the same unity that Christ creates with the church, as Ephesians notes throughout. Yet even in this profound marriage between Christ and the church, there can be confusion and disagreement. When Jesus tells his disciples that they will eat his flesh and drink his blood, they respond, "This teaching is difficult; who can accept it?" It is only by being subject and open to the Spirit that we are able to grasp Jesus' teaching, that it brings us to life. Openness to the other, even when understanding is missing, brings about unity.

When asked if they too wished "to go away," Peter answered Jesus, "Lord, to whom can we go? You have the words of eternal life." But in order to bring this unity to the church, Christ himself, subject to the will of the Father, offered himself for us. Our unity is not a participation in an object, but subjection to the "head of the church, the body of which he is the Savior."

Consider your feelings and thoughts when thinking about the nature of "subjection." How have you seen these passages from Ephesians be misused in people's relationships? Have you seen instances in which these passages have been properly understood? Whether as church or in personal relationships, how can we be properly subject to one another?

JUST DO IT

Twenty-Second Sunday in Ordinary Time

Readings: Deut 4:1-2, 6-8; Ps 15:2-3, 3-4, 4-5;
Jas 1:17-18, 21b-22, 27; Mark 7:1-8, 14-15, 21-23

"But be doers of the word, and not merely hearers." (Jas 1:22)

The relationship of Christianity with the law has often been conflicted, stemming from the apostle Paul's complex teachings regarding the Torah and Jesus' own words, like those from the Gospel of Mark. There Jesus cites Isaiah to the Pharisees and scribes, "in vain do they worship me, / teaching human precepts as doctrines," and then adds, "You abandon the commandment of God and hold to human tradition." But note in Jesus' teaching that he does not deny the validity of "the commandment of God," but criticizes the abandonment of it for "teaching human precepts" or "human tradition."

The Christian reception of the Torah, God's law, is therefore confusing for Christians and others today. Many internet memes note that the church accepts some Old Testament laws, like the Ten Commandments and prohibitions regarding homosexual behavior, but not those about mixing fabrics or eating shellfish. While Jewish theology has never accepted a division in the Torah between moral laws and ceremonial laws, understanding all of the law as a seamless garment, later Christian theologians, like Thomas Aquinas, did so.

Yet these later discussions and distinctions, which understood certain Old Testament laws as fulfilled in Jesus' mission, should not allow us to treat our obedience to God's law as provisional or insignificant. As much as most of us hate to be told what to do regarding certain behaviors, this is precisely what God does.

Fine philosophical and theological distinctions regarding the law are not insignificant, but both Jesus and James, the brother of Jesus to whom the Letter of James is attributed, warn against a legal casuistry that renders moot the question of what God wants us to do.

Jesus warns us against our hearts being turned against God and our fellow humans, saying, "It is what comes out of a person that defiles. For it is from within, from the human heart, that evil intentions come: fornication, theft, murder, adultery, avarice, wickedness, deceit, licentiousness, envy, slander, pride, folly. All these evil things come from within, and they defile a person."

The starting point regarding excising sin is always a searching, personal moral inventory, since whenever we sin it is because we have given ourselves permission, in however subtle a way, to do what we desire. Just this once. No one will be the wiser. Who will know? I deserve this. After all, everyone does it! As Ronny Cammareri says in the movie *Moonstruck*, "I ain't no freakin' monument to justice!"

The Letter of James continues Jesus' theme of converting our own hearts in order to follow God's law. James writes, "Let everyone be quick to listen, slow to speak, slow to anger; for your anger does not produce God's righteousness. Therefore rid yourselves of all sordidness and rank growth of wickedness, and welcome with meekness the implanted word that has the power to save your souls." The phrase "implanted word" (*emphytos logos*) suggests Scripture, naturally, but at an even deeper level of growth suggests that our source of conversion is Jesus, the Word (*Logos*) made flesh, planted in us, able to root us and ground us in God's ways, which are found in Scripture.

For Jesus is not just the Word made flesh but the law (*nomos*) made flesh. As James goes on to say, "Those who look into the perfect law, the law of liberty, and persevere, being not hearers who forget but doers who act—they will be blessed in their doing." This perfect law (*nomon teleion*) is Jesus himself, and Jesus offers a law of freedom, *eleutheria*, which seems initially to be a contradiction. How can the law that restrains us give us freedom?

The law of freedom indicates that doing God's law fulfills human desires perfectly, blessing us, since it responds to our deepest needs regarding who we are and what we are intended to become. James says that if we do not do the word, but only hear it, we "are like those who look at themselves in a mirror; for they look at themselves and, on going away, immediately forget what they were like." Why? Because we only become who we are intended to be by doing what God wants us to do. We come to know ourselves by understanding God's law, our purpose for ourselves. We know ourselves by just doing it.

Listen to the teaching of Jesus and James. What is your response to law? Do you see it as freeing or constraining? How does your freedom in Christ guide you in all that you do?

Be Strong; Do Not Fear

Twenty-Third Sunday in Ordinary Time

Readings: Isa 35:4-7a; Ps 146:7, 8-9, 9-10;
Jas 2:1-5; Mark 7:31-37

*"The LORD watches over the strangers; /
he upholds the orphan and the widow."* (Ps 146:9)

How can people be upset about a lion being killed, even if it was lured out of a protected area and slaughtered? A lion? There are babies being killed throughout the country, the world even, and people are upset about animals? Why is Planned Parenthood not at the top of the news? But what about human lives after conception, do these lives matter at all? Do #BlackLivesMatter? Do the lives of migrants drowning in the Mediterranean matter to anyone?

To protest about one sort of injustice does not mean that people consider other injustices irrelevant. Expressing moral outrage over animals and their environment need not be at odds with defending the lives of innocent babies in the womb whose lives are brutally ended or with neighbors whose lives are at risk daily from racism, manifested in numerous ways, but most clearly in white supremacist rhetoric that leads even to the mass murder of black Christians praying in the quiet of a church. One can act on behalf of migrants making their way to Europe on the flimsiest of vessels and still speak out about the incarceration rate in US prisons.

While each of us has limited time and energy and will have to choose to which of these various injustices we will lend our voice and effort toward healing, we are not engaged in some sort of zero-sum game of indignation, in which one cause must rule them all. As Pope Francis has written of St. Francis of Assisi in *Laudato Sì* (2015), "He shows us just how inseparable the bond is between concern for nature, justice for the poor, commitment to society, and interior peace" (10). They are not odd pieces of a puzzle that will not fit together but integral pieces that are all necessary for the puzzle to come together.

But what of another piece of the puzzle, the interior peace of which Pope Francis speaks? How does outrage lend itself to interior peace? This is where it is important to see outrage as a manifestation of that inchoate desire for justice, implanted in us so deeply by God, which itself needs purpose and goal. Our outrage reflects our desire for justice, but the desire for justice needs hope to flourish. It needs the promise, "Be strong, do not fear! / Here is your God. / He will come with vengeance, / with terrible recompense. / He will come and save you."

We must cry out for the oppressed, weep for the loss of innocent life, and act justly in response to injustice, but we must never forget to pray in hope. God has not forgotten and God will not forget. Our hope for justice is an inkling of God's will, "who executes justice for the oppressed; / who gives food to the hungry. / The LORD sets the prisoners free; / the LORD opens the eyes of the blind. / The LORD lifts up those who are bowed down; / the LORD loves the righteous. / The LORD watches over the strangers; / he upholds the orphan and the widow, / but the way of the wicked he brings to ruin." God has not suddenly turned his back on the prisoners, the weak, and the oppressed or forgotten the ways of wickedness. God calls us to be strong, to not fear, and to act with hope.

As we act, we know that God is with us. Action begins at home, says James, by not making distinctions among the poor and the rich at church, treating the "poor person in shabby clothes" with disdain and "the one wearing the fine clothes" with honor. Think of Jesus' ministry, how ordinary and mundane it was in many ways, reaching out to individuals as he walked a particular and small patch of this earth. Jesus responded to human need and suffering around him by healing a deaf man, feeding the hungry—each person of value in God's plan to redeem humanity. That plan of redemption has not come to an end, and we can act in concert with it, for "the God who created the universe out of nothing can also intervene in this world and overcome every form of evil. Injustice is not invincible" (*Laudato Sì* 74). Indeed, God's word is clear: true justice is our hope and destiny.

Though we can feel overwhelmed by injustice and sin in the world, God asks us to have hope. How can you act in response to injustice? Pray for guidance so that you may implement justice more fully in your life, in your community, and in your country.

THE THINGS OF GOD

Twenty-Fourth Sunday in Ordinary Time

Readings: Isa 50:4c-9a; Ps 116:1-2, 3-4, 5-6, 8-9;
Jas 2:14-18; Mark 8:27-35

"For you are setting your mind . . . on human things." (Mark 8:33)

Jesus bluntly rebukes Peter, telling him, "You are setting your mind not on divine things but on human things." There are two contexts for this rebuke: one is the particular circumstance in which Peter himself rebuked Jesus for revealing his passion; and the other is the general human reality in which all people struggle to understand the division of human things and divine things.

In the first context, an interesting question is, What did Peter actually say to Jesus? Given that Jesus has just disclosed that "the Son of Man must undergo great suffering, and be rejected by the elders, the chief priests, and the scribes, and be killed, and after three days rise again," it is not a stretch to believe that Peter rejected the need for the Son of Man to suffer and die. Jesus' divinely ordained and freely chosen destiny is, in this context, the "divine things" (the Greek is literally "the things of God," *ta tou theou*).

More concretely, though, what might these "human things" ("the things of human beings," *ta tōn anthrōpōn*) be? What are the things that draw us away from God's ways and desires? Although "human things" in themselves are not necessarily negative—avoiding suffering and death is not inherently wrong—what seems to be the case is that whenever (divine) values and (human) preferences come into conflict, one chooses the "divine thing." Values and preferences are not always at odds, but when they are, the choice must be made for the things of God.

What things did Peter tell Jesus to choose? When we reflect on Peter telling Jesus to choose the "human thing," it is hard to avoid considering the concrete temptations Satan offered Jesus in the Synoptic Gospel narratives, since it is Jesus who raises the specter of Satan here in Caesarea Philippi. It seems likely that Jesus does not consider Peter as Satan, but that the temptations Peter offers in the guise of helping Jesus are connected to the temptations of Satan that we know from Matthew and Luke—that is, the basic temptations that underlie all "human things."

In the temptation accounts, Jesus is offered the power to satisfy all his earthly hungers, the power to presume upon God's will and favor, and the power over all kingdoms. Wealth, authority, and fame—what more could a person want? Did Peter tempt Jesus with a plea for him not to die at the hands of foreign oppressors, the Romans, but to institute God's kingdom by conquering them militarily and installing himself as king? While it is impossible to know precisely what temptation Peter called upon Jesus to accept, it is not too much to believe that he asked him to act on his power and authority and bring about the kingdom of God in a way that aligned with "human things," that involved shows of force, might, and revenge.

When Peter identified Jesus as the Messiah, he must have had particular ideas not just of what this meant for the Messiah, God's Anointed One, but for those who were the Messiah's closest friends, his apostles and disciples. Whatever kingdom Peter's mind conjured, it probably did not involve denying himself and taking up his cross to follow Jesus or losing his life for the Gospel. What kind of kingdom is that? Feel for Peter for a moment. What kind of ridiculous kingdom is built on the broken body of a defeated Messiah?

This is the kingdom of "divine things," the kingdom of paradox. Tomáš Halík, the Czech priest and theologian, says, "If we have never had the feeling that what Jesus wants of us is absurd, crazy, and impossible, then we've probably either been too hasty in taming or diluting the radical nature of his teaching by means of soothing intellectualizing interpretations, or (mostly naïvely, illusorily, or even hypocritically) we have too easily forgotten just to what extent—in our thinking, customs, and actions—we are rooted 'in this world' where totally different rules apply" (*Night of the Confessor* [New York: Random House, 2012], 27). Jesus offers us the things of God, the things in which we save our lives by losing them and build a kingdom whose divine power is seen as human weakness.

Jesus speaks very bluntly to Peter about the things of God and the things of human beings. As Jesus speaks to you about divine and human things, does it seem too difficult to follow God? Do you have any questions for Jesus? How do you balance the things of God and the things of human beings?

THe GreaTesT

Twenty-Fifth Sunday in Ordinary Time

Readings: Wis 2:12, 17-20; Ps 54:3-4, 5, 6-8;
Jas 3:16–4:3; Mark 9:30-37

*"But they were silent, for on the way they had argued
with one another who was the greatest."* (Mark 9:34)

It feels good to belong—to one's family, to a group of friends, to a
team—to be part of something bigger than oneself. Belonging creates
feelings of comfort, joy, peace, and purpose. How good must it have felt
to be chosen as one of the twelve apostles? And to have an inkling, then
the growing certainty that the one who chose you is not just a man but
the Son of Man, the Messiah. The one who called you to be among the
inner circle, to be at the heart of the kingdom-building project, was the
one prophesied throughout the ages.

Whatever the ancient Jewish equivalent was of the fist-bump or the
"Yes!" while you high-five someone, it's hard not to imagine the apostles
getting a little pumped up about being the chosen Twelve.

This is the general context for understanding their behavior on the way
through Galilee, when Jesus was telling them, "The Son of Man is to be
betrayed into human hands, and they will kill him, and three days after
being killed, he will rise again." The Gospel of Mark tells us that they did
not understand what Jesus was saying and that they "were afraid to ask
him."

Was this fear simply a desire not to hear Jesus, not to distract from their
own scenarios of the future? It turns out that they had been arguing among
themselves about "who was the greatest." But this is normal, isn't it? "I
don't want to be a football player, I want to be the greatest football player!"
"I don't want to be an ordinary baker, I want to bake the greatest loaf of
bread this city has seen." And it does not seem inherently problematic to
want to fulfill one's human abilities and gifts to the best of one's ability.

So what is the problem with arguing, "I am not just one of the Twelve,
I am the greatest apostle"? Jesus presents to his apostles a spiritual world

121

in which true greatness is measured not by human striving or boundless ambition but by servanthood. This is a gift and an ability that does not rely on preeminence or superiority but on presence for those in need.

It is in caring for the little ones, Jesus says, that his apostles live up to the call of the Gospel. Jesus offers as an example a "little child" (*paidion*) and says, "Whoever welcomes one such child in my name welcomes me, and whoever welcomes me welcomes not me but the one who sent me." The treatment of the child becomes the measure of greatness because it demands true humility and service. Loving a child does not offer prestige, honor, or wealth, especially when a *paidion* in antiquity was generally in the care of mothers, nurses, or slaves. This was not the work of a man, certainly not the hand-picked viceroys of the Messiah.

Yet the deep wisdom of God is at work here, for we are all children of God, dependent at all points in our lives on the service of others, in varying and different ways. Spiritual humility is not the manifestation of a lack of self-esteem or a sense that we are unloved and unlovable but the acknowledgment that we are dependent upon God and others, even for the genuine gifts and vocations we are to express for others. Our boast must be that we are children of the Lord and that God is our father.

To recognize that we are called as disciples of Jesus is to be at the service of others, especially children and all others who are vulnerable, marginalized, and otherwise forgotten. Servanthood orients our relationships with others, for when our desires are out of order, as James writes, our relationships become disordered: "Those conflicts and disputes among you, where do they come from? Do they not come from your cravings that are at war within you?"

We fulfill these cravings when we belong, when we are loved, and when we are part of something. Jesus calls us to the church for this purpose, to care for those whose own hopes for belonging have been dashed. When we bring our manifold human gifts to the service of others, true greatness emerges with every act of love and every word of compassion.

We all yearn to belong, to be known and loved, but sometimes this can devolve into unbridled ambition, desire for human greatness, and even fear that we are unlovable. How do you understand greatness in the context of the kingdom of God and God's love for us? How can you demonstrate the greatness of those considered "little ones" by your society?

THe CHallenGe OF THe WorD

Twenty-Sixth Sunday in Ordinary Time

Readings: Num 11:25-29; Ps 19:8, 10, 12-13, 14;
Jas 5:1-6; Mark 9:38-43, 45, 47-48

*"Would that all the Lord's people were prophets,
and that the Lord would put his spirit on them!"* (Num 11:29)

Although a knowledge of history, ancient languages, and the culture and society of ancient Israel and the Roman Empire are helpful for biblical interpretation, ordinary readers, without any of these scholarly tools, sometimes get to the heart of the meaning of biblical passages far more quickly and acutely than experts.

The academic expertise necessary to study the Bible professionally—knowledge of Hebrew, Greek, archaeology, textual criticism, and rabbinic Judaism—takes years to accumulate and can lead to profound insights into the Bible and the biblical world. So what holds expert readers of the Bible from understanding the Bible?

Bernard Lonergan, SJ, said that what was necessary for both professional and everyday readers to truly understand the Bible was conversion, by which he meant intellectual, moral, and religious conversion. Religious conversion for readers of the Bible is, however, essential, for it is "the transition from the horizon of this-worldly commitments to the primacy in one's life of the love of God" (Ben F. Meyer, *Critical Realism and the New Testament* [Eugene, OR: Wipf and Stock, 1989], 69). Unless an interpreter is "in tune" with the world of the text and in love with God, the tools of the expert do not always bear fruit.

Why does such an esoteric discussion matter? It matters because it is not truly an esoteric discussion. The Bible is not primarily a playground for professionals or experts but for disciples who want to guide their life according to its teachings, and it matters that every Christian reads the Bible "in tune" with God's spirit.

Reading the Bible is the means by which we come to witness God's activities among the Israelites and read of God's Spirit working among them. We learn that Moses said, "Would that all the LORD's people were prophets, and that the LORD would put his spirit on them!" We learn, that is, that God's spirit is not intended for a few members of the elite but for each woman, man, and child.

We learn also of the false gospel of current prosperity preachers from our encounter with James, who says, "Come now, you rich people, weep and wail for the miseries that are coming to you. Your riches have rotted, and your clothes are moth-eaten." It challenges us not because the interpretation of the passage is difficult but because so many of us are rich and want to find a way to soften the clear message directed at us. True interpreters ask not to change the Bible to our liking, but to be transformed by God's spirit challenging our ways.

God does not desire the proper academic curriculum vitae, but saving behavior, since "whoever gives you a cup of water to drink because you bear the name of Christ will by no means lose the reward. If any of you put a stumbling block before one of these little ones who believe in me, it would be better for you if a great millstone were hung around your neck and you were thrown into the sea." We find in the gospel that God wants us to care for the weak, to sustain the "little ones who believe in me," to offer justice. God asks us to live our faith, to nurture the vulnerable, not just talk about the faith or interpret it.

And God promises, we learn in the Bible, that there are consequences for our behavior, a promise of judgment, where we will be called to give an account for our behavior, perhaps now or in the future, in a place called Gehenna or, as it is often translated into English, hell.

For all of these reasons, biblical interpretation is too important to leave to the experts, though experts have much of value to say, because understanding the Bible concerns our eternity. Our ability to understand the truth of the Bible depends on our willingness to hear all of the Bible's message, especially the passages that trouble and challenge us, because that is where conversion is often most necessary. Conversion turns us from being hearers of the Bible to doers, and from experts in interpretation to experts in hearing the voice of God in our daily lives.

Sometimes we fall back on ways of understanding the Bible that are comfortable to us or do not challenge us. When you read the Bible, what passages challenge you the most? How is God troubling you to live your life according to the Gospel? How has the Bible led to conversion in your life?

LITTLE CHILDREN OF THE WORD

Twenty-Seventh Sunday in Ordinary Time

Readings: Gen 2:18-24; Ps 128:1-2, 3, 4-5, 6;
Heb 2:9-11; Mark 10:2-16

*"Truly I tell you, whoever does not receive the kingdom of God
as a little child will never enter it."* (Mark 10:15)

In his teaching on divorce, Jesus claims that the circumstances that allowed for divorce in the Mosaic law were due to the "hardness of heart" of human beings after the fall. These laws were conditional, Jesus says, not God's intent "from the beginning of creation." Jesus cites passages from Genesis that reflect the human condition prior to the fall from Paradise. In the Garden, "God made them male and female," reflecting Genesis 1:27, with the intent that "a man leaves his father and his mother and clings to his wife, and they become one flesh" (Gen 2:24).

In his teaching on marriage, therefore, Jesus is directing us to the beginning, what is called in German theology the *Urzeit*, the time prior to human sin. What are the grounds for Jesus' statement that his followers are once again in the time of the beginning? What are the signs that it is Paradise now? Jesus himself, the Word made flesh, "who for a little while was made lower than the angels," is the sign.

The German biblical scholar Lutz Doering writes that in Jesus' teaching "what we encounter . . . is a model of restoration of paradisiacal conditions in the kingdom of God, an *Urzeit-Endzeit* correlation" ("Marriage and Creation in Mark 10 and CD 4-5," in *Echoes from the Caves: Qumran and the New Testament* [Boston: Brill, 2009], 158). For with Jesus comes the inauguration of the kingdom of God, the beginning of the *eschaton*, or *Endzeit*, when God will make all things new. It is only with the coming of the Messiah that we can hope to be transformed into people of the kingdom, capable of following God's intent "from the beginning of creation."

It is true, of course, that we do not live in the Garden of Eden now. Every sin of our own wayward hearts, every sign of sin and destruction in the world makes that obvious to us all. And yet Jesus tells us that the conditions have changed. The *Endzeit* has been inaugurated with the coming of the kingdom, because the Messiah came to live among us and to allow us to follow his way, established by Jesus to bring "many children to glory . . . for the one who sanctifies and those who are sanctified all have one Father. For this reason Jesus is not ashamed to call them brothers and sisters." Jesus, our brother, has come to bring us to our true, native home, but also to show us how we must live there.

The pathway home was not obvious to Jesus' first disciples, who asked Jesus "again about this matter" of marriage and divorce. Jesus instructed them further regarding these things, but one might argue he instructs them more significantly by indicating the change of heart necessary to enter the kingdom and to live according to the ways of the kingdom. The kingdom is about transformation, about conversion of intellect, heart, and soul.

At the end of the discourse about marriage and divorce, the disciples want to send away people who were bringing children to Jesus, "and the disciples spoke sternly to them." This, however, is not the way of the kingdom but of the fallen world. Jesus "was indignant" with the disciples, saying, "Let the little children come to me; do not stop them; for it is to such as these that the kingdom of God belongs. Truly I tell you, whoever does not receive the kingdom of God as a little child will never enter it."

What it means to "receive the kingdom of God as a little child" is surely complex. Or is it? Is Jesus' point that as little children accept Jesus, and the ways of God, with vulnerability, openness, freedom, innocence, guilelessness, not to gain anything, not to calculate wins and losses, but simply to accept the kingdom for what it is, so we must accept the kingdom? If we are being taken back to the *Urzeit*, to Paradise restored in the *Endzeit*, then we are being taken to a time of primal innocence, in which the love of the other, in marriage as well as all of our other relationships, is grounded in God's perfection. Surely none of us is perfect now; but the kingdom calls for transformation, to become like a "little child," and the one who calls us will surely bring us home.

Not just marriage but many relationships can break down because of our own fallen ways. How can we, by allowing ourselves to be transformed, help to restore our relationships? How can we become like "little children" as we grow in the ways of the kingdom? What does it mean to you to receive God's kingdom as a "little child"?

THE SPIRIT OF WISDOM

Twenty-Eighth Sunday in Ordinary Time

Readings: Wis 7:7-11; Ps 90:12-13, 14-15, 16-17;
Heb 4:12-13; Mark 10:17-30

"I called on God, and the spirit of wisdom came to me." (Wis 7:7)

An elected county clerk in Rowan County, Kentucky, Kim Davis, was jailed for refusing to grant marriage licenses. She is required by law to offer marriage licenses to same-sex couples, which she refused to do since it affronts her understanding of the nature of marriage as a Christian. The situation has riled up many people. Some consider her a martyr who is being persecuted for her religious beliefs; others consider her a hypocrite for refusing to do her elected duty, especially since she herself has been divorced three times. While numerous evangelical Christians support her, Catholic commentators have also defended her, on the basis of Scripture and natural law, specifically the principle that an unjust law is no law at all and might even demand civil disobedience.

This dispute has become a source of rancor among Christians because it exposes deep cultural fault lines about the relationship of civil law to divine mandates. But while the particular issue might be new, Christian allegiance to divine commands in the face of contrary civil law has a long history, grounded not only in the teaching of the apostles and the behavior of the first martyrs but also among Jews like the Maccabees and the figure of Daniel. The well-formed conscience has a genuine integrity that cannot be dismissed with snide remarks or by harshly judging the authenticity of participants in a dispute.

How does one navigate contentious issues? What is needed is wisdom. Wisdom, *sophia* in Greek, *hochmah* in Hebrew, is personified in Scripture as a divine figure who comes from God to guide us. "Therefore I prayed," says the Wisdom of Solomon, "and understanding was given me; / I called on God, and the spirit of wisdom came to me." We are told that wisdom must be valued above all human gains—"I preferred her to scepters and

thrones, / and I accounted wealth as nothing in comparison with her"—
but that with wisdom "all good things came to me along with her, / and
in her hands uncounted wealth."

Wisdom can take time to find and counsel us, and wisdom requires our
attention. In these days, filled with more distractions than ever before, we
are called to make complex moral judgments in an instant. Yet the psalmist
prays, "Teach us to count our days / that we may gain a wise heart."
Wisdom is not the product of the wittiest tweet, the snarkiest put-down,
or the cleverest meme but the fruit of prayer, reflection, and humility.

Wisdom means carefully examining the positions of others, especially
when we are convinced we are correct. Wisdom asks us to see the human
beings behind the sound bites, searching out their humanity, even when
we are convinced their stance is wrongheaded.

As Christians, we have Scripture to introduce us to wisdom, and we
know that "the word of God is living and active, sharper than any two-
edged sword, piercing until it divides soul from spirit, joints from marrow;
it is able to judge the thoughts and intentions of the heart." Wisdom comes
through attentive reading, when we allow Scripture to interrogate our
hearts and minds.

When we read with the teaching and tradition of the church, we are
able to hear the wisdom of the people of God and the magisterium, and
it is more than just a process of looking to the correct page and chapter in
the catechism. Think of Jesus, who met a man who had followed all the
commandments exactly, but when Jesus asked him to sell what he owned
and to give the money to the poor so that he would "have treasure in
heaven; then come, follow me," the man balked at accepting Jesus' wisdom, as most of us might.

Peter, too, cried out to Jesus after the rich young man left, "Look, we
have left everything and followed you!" Jesus was challenging his disciples to look beyond commandments simply as a form of proper proce-
dure to the value of wisdom, "uncounted wealth," "treasure in heaven,"
which can guide us in the most tumultuous of times to eternal life.

Free yourself from distractions and seek out wisdom. What difficult social
issues or church teaching demand your prayers and reflections? What
helps you to make certain you are seeking out wisdom, the eternal treasure, and not simply your own way? Where do you go for the source of
your wisdom?

suffering servant

"Whoever wishes to be first among you must be slave of all."
(Mark 10:44)

In chapters 40 to 55 of Isaiah, there are four passages known as the Servant Songs. One of them, quoted as today's first reading, is about the Suffering Servant. One wonders what it was like to read about this Suffering Servant in Isaiah, where we hear, "it was the will of the LORD to crush him with pain," apart from an encounter with the life and death of Jesus. How were these verses understood, in which we are told, "The righteous one, my servant, shall make many righteous, / and he shall bear their iniquities," before the disciples read them in light of Jesus' passion and resurrection?

Some modern scholars have proposed that the servant in Isaiah might represent the nation of Israel or the prophets; others identify the servant with an individual, like the prophet Isaiah himself, the Persian king Cyrus, or the future Messiah. As for the earliest disciples of Jesus, they were certain that the servant was the prophesied Messiah, who had lived, died, and been raised among them. Jesus was the one who was crushed, who bore our iniquities, and who "out of his anguish" saw "the light" in his resurrection.

Jesus' suffering and death were not, as the disciples had initially feared, the destruction of their hopes, but the fulfillment of divine hope. This allowed for heightened reflection to take place on the life of the Messiah, who had walked among them as they read the Law and the Prophets. This reflection upon Jesus, in light of the Hebrew Scriptures, is the foundation of the New Testament.

The Letter to the Hebrews, for instance, reflected upon Jesus as both human and divine, as the perfect Victim and the perfect High Priest, "who in every respect has been tested as we are, yet without sin." Because of Jesus' humanity and his suffering on our behalf, we have a Messiah who is able to "sympathize with our weaknesses." It is this sympathy, born of his incarnation and passion, that allowed Jesus to guide the earliest followers, the kernel of the church, into an understanding of the shared mission the apostles were to carry to the world.

Understanding was not always easy. When Jesus told his apostles that he must suffer and die, James and John find it the proper time to say, "Teacher, we want you to do for us whatever we ask of you." Jesus does not respond by asking them if they had even heard what he said but asks them, "What is it you want me to do for you?" The brothers Zebedee want "to sit, one at your right hand and one at your left, in your glory." Their answer establishes at least this much: They know Jesus is the Messiah, and they know he will establish God's kingdom. The problem is one of misunderstanding, not just because Jesus has announced his coming death for the third time but because they desire glory without the suffering. They will not hear what Jesus has to say: the kingdom will come, but the Messiah must first suffer and die.

Jesus says to be a leader in the church is not to be a "lord" or "tyrant." Jesus' goal is not to replace Gentile lords and tyrants with new, improved Jewish lords and tyrants, but in the kingdom, or "reign" of God, rulers must be servants; and "whoever wishes to be first among you must be slave of all." This is not empty language for the troops from a general who surveys the suffering on the battlefield from the safety of a mountaintop but from one who will suffer for them.

Jesus says that "the Son of Man came not to be served but to serve, and to give his life as a ransom for many." In this verse Jesus interprets his death as a sacrificial death. The language of "ransom" evokes salvation through purchase, freeing "many" from slavery or capture. "Many" is the language of Isaiah 53:12, in which the servant "poured out himself to death . . . yet he bore the sin of many, / and made intercession for the transgressors." Jesus offers himself out of sympathy for our weakness, for the sake of humanity, which cannot save itself. I am this servant, Jesus says, are you willing to follow me and to serve me through service to all?

Think of Jesus' love for humanity, "sympathizing with our weakness," offering himself "for many." How do you respond to Jesus' life as the Suffering Servant? How can you live out Jesus' command to be a servant for all? How do you balance leadership and service?

THe Sum of Mercy

Thirtieth Sunday in Ordinary Time

Readings: Jer 31:7-9; Ps 126:1-2, 2-3, 4-5, 6;
Heb 5:1-6; Mark 10:46-52

"Jesus, Son of David, have mercy on me!" (Mark 10:47)

When Jesus encounters the blind man Bartimaeus, son of Timaeus, in Mark's gospel, he has just unveiled the last of the three passion predictions, in which he explains the suffering and death that await him in Jerusalem. Jesus is leaving Jericho on the way to his destiny in Jerusalem, and Bartimaeus is begging on the roadside. The identification of Bartimaeus, whose name in Aramaic means "son of Timaeus" and so encapsulates his father's name Timaeus as well, is unusually precise and detailed for Mark. It signals, therefore, an important encounter in Mark's narrative, though it might seem Jesus has more significant things on his mind.

The use of Bartimaeus's name indicates the historical dimension of this encounter and suggests that Bartimaeus became a disciple after his healing, since he "followed him on the way." The memory of the healing on the way to Jerusalem might also have remained especially significant in the minds of the disciples because of its timing, since in Mark it is the last of Jesus' healings during his ministry. But there is more to it than these convincing historical and narrative explanations. The importance of this encounter has to do with mercy.

When Bartimaeus hears that Jesus is on the road, "he began to shout out and say, 'Jesus, Son of David, have mercy on me!' " Bartimaeus understands Jesus' identity, for it is the first time in the gospel that anyone has identified Jesus as "the Son of David," one of the most significant of the messianic titles, connecting its bearer to the historical David and the Davidic kingship.

The response of the disciples is telling. "Many sternly ordered him to be quiet," and these many included Jesus' apostles and other followers. The verb used here, *epitimaō*, has the sense of scolding, rebuking, or censuring with contempt. People told him, basically, to shut up.

To Bartimaeus's credit, he would not listen, "but he cried out even more loudly, 'Son of David, have mercy on me!'" Why would you shut up if the Son of David is walking by? One wonders whether the fact that at this point, long into Jesus' ministry, disciples are still telling blind men who call to Jesus to leave him alone offers us a glimpse into their stubborn lack of understanding of Jesus' mission of mercy and the nature of their Messiah.

Bartimaeus has something these followers of Jesus' lack: the understanding that even if he is physically (and spiritually?) blind, he knows where to go for the cure. He has faith in the mercy of Jesus and he will not be put off by disciples shooing him away as a nuisance.

Jesus stops and tells his disciples to "call him here," so they go to the blind beggar saying, "Take heart; get up, he is calling you." Bartimaeus needs no further invitation, and "throwing off his cloak, he sprang up and came to Jesus." Jesus' question "What do you want me to do for you?" is more powerful when you imagine it visually rather than simply as words on the page. Remember, Bartimaeus has twice called out to the "Son of David" to "have mercy on me." What exactly could this blind man begging at the side of the road want?

Jesus knows exactly what he wants, what the sum of mercy is in this context, but he wants Bartimaeus to say it again, not for Jesus' sake or to exasperate Bartimaeus but for the sake of the disciples and the crowd, some of whom moments ago were telling him to be quiet, shut up, and leave the great man alone. Bartimaeus simply asks, "My teacher, let me see again." Jesus' response is just as direct: "Go; your faith has made you well." Bartimaeus's faith leads to Jesus' mercy, but Jesus' mercy leads to spiritual discipleship, not just physical sight, as Bartimaeus does not "go" but "followed him on the way."

Bartimaeus's discipleship is the result of Jesus' mercy and the reason why mercy must be at the heart of the church's mission. Who do we tell today to shut up, to quit bothering the Messiah? Bartimaeus at the side of the road is an example for all those at the margins of the church calling out to be heard: do not give up on Jesus; he will listen and heal those who call out to him.

Picture yourself as Bartimaeus at the side of the road calling out to Jesus. What mercy do you want Jesus to do for you? What mercy are you being called upon to show others? How can we live out Jesus' mercy more completely?

Hear, O Israel

Thirty-First Sunday in Ordinary Time

Readings: Deut 6:2-6; Ps 18:2-3, 3-4, 47, 51;
Heb 7:23-28; Mark 12:28b-34

"Hear, O Israel: The LORD is our God, the LORD alone." (Deut 6:4)

Jesus does not introduce another commandment for Israel and his disciples, but he focuses attention on two commandments that were already prominent in the Torah. The first that Jesus recites is "Hear, O Israel: The LORD is our God, the LORD alone. You shall love the LORD your God with all your heart, and with all your soul, and with all your might." The second, found in Leviticus 19:18, states, "you shall love your neighbor as yourself." In the Gospel of Mark, Jesus says after stating these two commandments, "There is no other commandment greater than these."

In stating these commandments, Jesus was speaking to a Jewish audience and answering in response to a Jewish interlocutor, a scribe. These were commandments for Israel to hear and by which to live. But by the time the gospels were written and read in communities of Jesus' disciples, these commandments were embedded in mixed, possibly majority Gentile, churches. These were commandments for all the world to hear and to live.

While it might shock us today, monotheism was not the standard position in the ancient world. The world was peopled with gods, not just one God. Israel's belief, that there was only one, true, living God, was a minority position. The Romans, the Greeks, the Arabians, the Egyptians, all of the nations, had numerous gods and goddesses. The fact that early Christian disciples, such as Paul, Peter, Priscilla, and Aquila, asked people to turn from their gods and worship one God was a momentous change in the understanding of the nature of the world. It is so embedded in the world today that atheists usually take for granted monotheism; they reject one God, not many gods.

The Christian ministry of one God, already preached by the Jews, won the intellectual battle of antiquity, as well as the hearts and minds of people the world over. It made sense to people and continues to make sense to people today. The intellectual skirmishes over theism today are not fought between those who are polytheists and monotheists, but those who accept the truth of one God and those who reject the existence of one God.

Be that as it may, the second command to love one's neighbor, though equitable with the command to love God, and though more readily accepted and praised by people of all faiths or no faith, seems to falter in practice. While anyone can claim to love God, and who knows how well you or I do on any given day, the claim to love one's neighbor is something that is more visible to the world than our proclaimed love of God. When individual Christians or the church stumble in love of neighbor, everyone can see the results. This may be why Paul, who we can be certain knew of Deuteronomy 6:4 and Leviticus 19:18, as well as Jesus' oral tradition, states twice in his letters that we need to love our neighbors, but not once that we need to love God in the same contexts.

In Galatians 5:14 and Romans 13:9, Paul writes only that the whole law is fulfilled in the command to "love your neighbor as yourself." Why? I believe that Paul assumed that his churches truly loved God, but that making that love manifest in the world demanded the much harder task of striving to love our neighbor who often frustrates or upsets us. It is not always easy to love our neighbor even if it is the fulfillment of the whole law.

This is precisely the reason for the incarnation, so that the whole world would know not just to love God, but have a model for love of neighbor in the person of Jesus Christ. The Letter to the Hebrews describes Jesus as "holy, blameless, undefiled, separated from sinners, and exalted above the heavens." But this same Jesus, a High Priest unlike other high priests, took on human flesh to be for us the model of love of neighbor. As God's son, "a Son who has been made perfect forever," he offered himself once for all out of love for humanity, showing us the path for love of neighbor.

This is our daily work, to love God who gave himself for us and to love our neighbor as God loved us. These are not new—God gave these commands to the Israelites—but through the teaching of Jesus and his church they have become the heart of the law for the Gentiles. Hear, everyone, the commands we are to follow, ancient and new: to love God and to love our neighbors. But what a benefit we have today, for God tells us not only the commands, but has offered us a Savior who fulfilled them in the pouring out of his life.

Meditate on the commands to love God and to love neighbor. How do you struggle and fulfill the command to love God? How do you struggle and fulfill the command to love your neighbor? What can you do today to more fully show your love for God and neighbor?

WIDOWS anD scriBes

Thirty-Second Sunday in Ordinary Time

Readings: 1 Kgs 17:10-16; Ps 146:7, 8-9, 9-10;
Heb 9:24-28; Mark 12:38-44

*"A poor widow came and put in two small copper coins,
which are worth a penny."* (Mark 12:42)

Concerns about the economic teachings of Pope Francis, that he is a
Marxist for instance, are bandied about whenever he criticizes unfettered
capitalism. These concerns ought to be forwarded to a higher source, since
the pope's critique stems not from modern political divisions but from
the biblical call to offer justice to those in need. For it is God "who executes
justice for the oppressed; / who gives food to the hungry. . . . He upholds
the orphan and the widow, / but the way of the wicked he brings to ruin."

The prophet Elijah demonstrates God's concern for those economically
oppressed when he goes to see the widow of Zarephath, a single mother,
and asks for water and bread. The request seems thoughtless initially, for
the widow has only a little food for her and her son, and it is about to run
out. She asks Elijah to let her "go home and prepare it for myself and my
son, that we may eat it, and die."

Elijah instructs her to make the food as she had planned, but he asks
that she "first make me a little cake." Elijah promises her that God has
spoken and her food will be abundant, that she will not run out of grain
or oil. The widow prepared what little food she had for the prophet and,
true to God's word, she was rewarded with an abundance. The clarity of
the widow of Zarephath giving all to God and being rewarded with abundance is, however, muddied in the gospel account of another widow, who
gives all of her money to the temple treasury.

Just prior to this passage, Jesus has said, "Beware of the scribes," who
"devour widows' houses and for the sake of appearance say long prayers.
They will receive the greater condemnation." Immediately after giving
this warning, Jesus sits down by the treasury and watches "many rich

people put in large sums." Then "a poor widow came and put in two small copper coins, which are worth a penny." Jesus tells his disciples that "this poor widow has put in more than all those who are contributing to the treasury. For all of them have contributed out of their abundance; but she out of her poverty has put in everything she had, all she had to live on."

Whereas Elijah asks for a little sustenance from the widow and returns God's generosity to her and her son in abundance, here the widow has given "all she had to live on," and it is not clear what she will receive from God's representatives at the temple.

There are two ways to look at her action. The first, in light of the story of the widow of Zarephath, is that since she has given all to God, she will likewise be rewarded, even if Jesus does not mention this. She demonstrated a love of God and love of neighbor by giving all she had to the temple treasury. By doing so, she has acted on her belief that God will care for her and that she will rely on her neighbors to make God's care for her known in her life.

The second is that this is an instance of how "widows' houses" are devoured by taking advantage of her religious piety. While the widow models "giving until it hurts," who will supply her economic needs now or ameliorate her pain? Is Jesus praising her action by drawing attention to it or grieving that no one else would give all for God's sake? Has the widow's religiosity been exploited? Should it be the temple and those who serve the temple—or, in our context today, the church and those who serve the church—who give to the poor widow? We know that God gave abundantly to the widow of Zarephath through Elijah, but who will supply this widow's economic needs?

Jesus is not focused on simply criticizing first-century Jewish scribes. After all, earlier a scribe is described by Jesus as "not far from the kingdom of God" (Mark 12:34). But Jesus is drawing our attention to the fact that it is the duty of God's representatives to serve those in need. The issue for Christians today is to ask not only how we might model the widow's generosity to God but how we can imitate God's generosity toward the widow and those like her who have given all to God's service.

Reflect on the widow giving all that she had. How do you emulate her generosity? How do you care for those most in need? What more can you do for those in poverty, personally and systemically?

NOW or THEN

Thirty-Third Sunday in Ordinary Time

Readings: Dan 12:1-3; Ps 16:5, 8, 9-10, 11;
Heb 10:11-14, 18; Mark 13:24-32

"But about that day or hour no one knows." (Mark 13:32)

When Jesus outlines the apocalyptic scenario found in the Gospel of Mark, he warns, "But about that day or hour, no one knows, neither the angels in heaven, nor the Son, but only the Father." Patristic discussion of this verse focused on what this admission indicated about Jesus' divinity and the relationship between Jesus' divine and human knowledge, but in context the intent of this saying points to the need for vigilance and perseverance regarding the coming end, since no one knows when it will occur.

But Jesus also tells us in Mark that "this generation will not pass away until all these things have taken place." The sense of imminence here is profound, though later Christians would argue whether Jesus meant the generation of his disciples or the generation of all human beings, while others discussed whether "all these things" referred to Jesus' death and resurrection, the destruction of Jerusalem, or "the Son of Man coming in clouds with great power and glory," which is the clearest meaning.

The themes of imminent preparation for the end, the *eschaton*, and the fact that no one knows when the end will occur, therefore, have been joined in Christianity from the earliest days, maintaining a tension between what has been accomplished (realized eschatology) and what is still to come (future eschatology).

Whether we understand, or believe we understand, much about the last things—not only when these things will occur but what sort of process we go through in death; what the interim period between our death and the resurrection is like; the process of purgatory; what the heavenly life is like, whether it takes place on a renewed earth or in a heavenly, otherworldly domain—these mysteries will in many ways remain mysteries on this side of death and appear to us as vague and incomplete.

We have the assurances of revelation, however, that there is a world to come and that it may come in fullness at any time. Daniel, in the most explicit verses of the Old Testament, tells us that there will be a general resurrection at the end of time and that the dead will rise, "some to everlasting life, and some to shame and everlasting contempt." In a compact passage we are told of the reality of what is still to come.

In an odd way, though, the dramatic and mythic apocalyptic scenarios of the coming end can be distractions from the realities to which they point: death, judgment, heaven, and hell—the four last things. How? Calculating the end times and whether the apocalypse will play out now or then, in this way or that, can draw us away from preparation for our own end.

For death is coming for each of us, whether we will confront it in our own personal *eschaton* or in the cosmic apocalyptic drama as described in the Gospel of Mark. Even if "the end" does not occur in our lifetime, and even if another group of end-time prophets falsely calculate Jesus' return and offer precise dates that do not come to pass, we will still come to our end. How are we preparing for it?

For this is not just a future reality. This is our life to live now and then. It is incumbent upon us to live for God, to begin the process of righteous living now that will be brought to perfection then, at the time of the end. Our time is short, even from the perspective of human history, but especially in the scope of eternity, and it can end at any time.

But as Jesus tells us, the time of the end is the coming of the Son of Man, the time of the fullness of revelation—the time, that is, when God makes all things new. And though it is true that apocalyptic scenarios speak of persecution and torment, this is not the final story, though modern apocalyptic movies, books, and video games give an inordinate and theologically unsound emphasis to darkness and desperation. Death can create fear for us, as do judgment and hell, but we were created for one last thing, heaven, to be like and to be with God. Jesus encourages us to prepare now, for this is the time to get ready for whatever happens and whenever it takes place.

Pray about the four last things. Is there something in particular you fear? Is there something confusing to you about the coming end? What comforts you as you reflect on Jesus' teachings about the end of time?

KING OF ALL

"My kingdom is not from this world." (John 18:36)

The political context in which Pope Pius XI, by the encyclical *Quas Primas*, established the feast of Christ the King in 1925 was the still unresolved Roman Question, which concerned the papacy and the kingdom of Italy regarding the temporal authority of the popes and the Papal States. For those of us who have grown up with the separation of church and state, the Papal States are a distant historical oddity.

Yet, even if these political issues no longer resonate for us today, *Quas Primas* commemorated these same issues and problems by taking the view that marks the church off as a unique society, one that is eternal, whose King's authority transcends all political divisions and historical epochs. The church exists in the messiness of history and responds to events that emerge from that same messiness but claims a King who transcends it all.

Already in the book of Daniel and in earlier prophetic books, the hope for the true king, the one who would establish God's kingdom, emerged in the language and imagery of ancient Near Eastern myth, when the prophet sees "one like a human being [son of man] / coming with the clouds of heaven." While scholars dispute the identification of the son of man as the messiah in Daniel, the earliest Christians understood that the one to whom "was given dominion / and glory and kingship, / that all peoples, nations, and languages / should serve him" was Jesus, whose "dominion is an everlasting dominion / that shall not pass away" and whose "kingship is one / that shall never be destroyed." This was the King of all.

When would this King of all peoples, nations, and languages arrive? When would God's kingdom, the everlasting dominion, be established? The book of Revelation, written in opposition to the Caesars of Rome and their empire, declared that Jesus was already "the ruler of the kings of the earth," who "made us to be a kingdom, priests serving his God and Father, to him be glory and dominion forever and ever." And Revelation promised, evoking the language of Daniel, that Jesus' first coming will be followed by a second coming with the clouds when "every eye will see him, / even those who pierced him; / and on his account all the tribes of the earth will wail."

Even Jesus' disciples, though, who followed him faithfully if unsurely to Jerusalem, must have wondered about the answer when they heard the Roman procurator Pilate ask their teacher, "Are you the King of the Jews?" Jesus answered, "My kingdom is not from this world. If my kingdom were from this world, my followers would be fighting to keep me from being handed over to the Jews. But as it is, my kingdom is not from here." It is a true answer, of course, but also elusive, for though Jesus' kingdom is "not from this world" and does not involve peace treaties, concordats, armies, and diplomatic corps, it includes all of this world and all that is in it.

It is a point Pope Pius XI makes in *Quas Primas* (13), citing Cyril of Alexandria, who wrote that "Christ has dominion over all creatures, a dominion not seized by violence nor usurped, but his by essence and by nature." Pius XI also writes that though Jesus' "kingship is founded upon the ineffable hypostatic union," Christ is also our King "by acquired, as well as by natural right, for he is our Redeemer." Jesus' kingship is unlike any other by nature and by behavior.

But there is another consideration as to why Jesus declared that his kingdom was "not from this world." Pius XI states that all people can enter this kingdom, whoever they are and from wherever they are since "this kingdom is opposed to none other than to that of Satan and to the power of darkness" (15). This kingdom welcomes all kingdoms and all people.

If we see only the messiness of history and politics, we are missing the true story of eternity and the true King of all, who is already "the ruler of the kings of the earth." If we believe it to be true, we must never despair of the politics of our age, for he came as King, is now King, and is coming again in glory.

Reflect on Christ as King. How does Jesus' kingship comfort you when you think of political and other disputes in our own day? Does the feast of Christ the King help you make sense of the church's role in the world? What does Christ's kingship mean to you as you go about your daily life?